Raising Kids to LOVE Being Jewish

Doron Kornbluth

THE KAPLAN-AGUIAR FAMILY EDITION

In Loving Memory of

Lillian Jean Kaplan

and

Otto Aguiar

Raising Kids to ✡ LOVE Being Jewish

K'hal
PUBLISHING

AFIKIM
FOUNDATION

Published by K'hal Publishing
In conjunction with The Afikim Foundation
111 John Street, Suite 1720
New York, NY 10038
212-791-7450
www.afikimfoundation.org

Layout & Design by Justine Elliott
Cover Design by BlockDesign/blockdesign@gmail.com

Distributed by MESORAH PUBLICATIONS, LTD.,
    4401 Second Avenue, Brooklyn, NY, 11232 www.artscroll.com
Distributed in Israel by SIFRATI/A. GITLER, 6 Hayarkon Street, Bnei Brak 51127
Distributed in Europe by LEHMANNS, Unit E, Viking Business Park,
    Rolling Mill Road, Jarrow, Tyne and Wear, NE32 3DP/England
Distributed in Australia and New Zealand by GOLDS WORLD OF JUDAICA,
    3-13 William Street, Balaclava, Melbourne 3183, Victoria, Australia
Distributed in South Africa by KOLLEL BOOKSHOP,
    Ivy Common, 105 William Road, Norwood 2192, Johannesburg, South Africa

ISBN: Hardcover 978-1-60204-015-1
    Paperback 978-1-60204-016-8

Printed in the United States of America.

CONTENTS

Acknowledgements

The idea for this work came from thousands of Jewish parents around the world who responded positively to my lectures on the subject.

Many friends and colleagues reviewed the manuscript and offered valuable suggestions toward its improvement. Critiquing a book is both difficult and time-consuming. To those who were able to make the time, at various periods over the years, I am much indebted. They include Dr. Lisa Aiken, David and Kerry Bar-Cohn, Rabbi Yaakov Blackman, Rabbi Menashe Bleiweiss, Rabbi Michael Cytrin, Tom Eisenstadt, Rabbi Avi Fine, Ian Freedman, Rabbi Dovid Goldman, Daniel Green, Gloria Greenfield, Rabbi Yehoshua Karsh, Rabbi Leib Kelemen, Rabbi Yehoshua Kohl, Dr. Bill Kolbrenner, Mrs. Faygie Matusof, Rabbi Yaakov Meyer, Donna Rader, Sara Yocheved Rigler, Mike Seid, Rabbi Gidon Shoshan, Joy Siegel, Dr. Ilene Sussman, Dr. Ilene Vogelstein, Dovid and Miriam Winiarz, Rabbi Pesach and Katie Wolicki, Rabbi Brad and Simi Yellen, and Rabbi Joel Zeff. My apologies – and gratitude—to anyone who was inadvertently left off of this list.

My parents, Harvey and Judy Kornbluth, have been incredibly supportive and encouraging of this work, as of all my endeavors. My in-laws, Jack and Joy Siegel, also deserve special mention for their significant help in a myriad of ways.

Rabbi Raphael Butler of K'hal Publishing and Rabbi Gedaliah Zlotowitz of ArtScroll / Mesorah Publications deserve much appreciation for their early recognition of the importance of this work and their encouragement along the way. Rabbi Shimon Apisdorf's skills as an editor and publisher have left a major positive impression on the book, and for that I am very grateful.

This book is the culmination of almost seven years of research, discussion, thought, writing, editing, and rewriting. It progressed at various speeds—sometimes a page a month, sometimes a page a day. Throughout, my wife's support has been fantastic. To say that my writing and lecturing would be impossible without her is an understatement: Without her I would have little to say.

Doron Kornbluth
JUNE 15, 2009

Introduction

I met Marty and Jen (not their real names) at the Los Angeles International Airport. I was flying to the East Coast and they were going to San Francisco. Our departure gates were beside each other and we struck up a conversation. After a few minutes, realizing our common Jewish identity, we unsuccessfully played some Jewish geography.

Both of them were Jewish, both were forced to go to Hebrew school, and neither of them liked it. Both were happy that Hebrew school ended with their Bar and Bat Mitzvah and neither had any Jewish education since. They simply had not been interested. Jewishness was not very significant in their homes growing up and was even less so now. Both had dated non-Jews for years, and religion was not a factor in choosing a partner – they only realized that they were both Jewish at the end of their second date!

They were not just flying to northern California – they were moving there. They both worked in Internet-based companies and could essentially work from anywhere. They wanted to plant roots in a place and be there for 20 or 30 years. They had done their research and chosen carefully – their destination was a ranch a couple of hours outside of San Francisco. No one lived in the vicinity at all. The area enjoyed a great climate. They wanted children, eventually, and there was a small town and a school within a 30 minute drive.

I asked if there was a Jewish community anywhere nearby. There wasn't—no community, no community center, no synagogue or Temple or High Holiday services. There weren't many people around at all, and as far as they knew there weren't even any other Jews.

1

There was so much I wanted to know and say. Were they consciously running away from their Jewishness? Or were they just uninterested? Did they want their children to know they were Jewish? To care? Had they thought about these issues at all?

Unfortunately, before I had a chance to ask any questions or offer any thoughts, their flight was ready for boarding and they got up to gather their belongings. We wished each other well and said goodbye.

I have often thought of Marty and Jen. Given more time, what could I have said?

The question goes beyond Marty and Jen. For thousands of Jewish couples and singles being Jewish is at most a minor part of their lives and they are unlikely to put any efforts into keeping their families Jewish. How can we explain to them—and ourselves—*why* it is important to keep our families Jewish and *how* to make it happen?

This is what I might have said to Marty and Jen and others like them.

Imagine you are in the largest room you have ever seen and that it is filled with millions of books.

You are not in a rush. You like books and enjoy walking through the stacks, choosing ones that seem interesting, sitting on a chair and reading, and getting lost in the thoughts of writers from contemporary times and ages past. You pick up whatever interests you and read for as long as you want. Once a book loses your interest, you move on to another, leaving the first to be read by someone else or perhaps ignored altogether. Each is just a book, and you have no obligation to start it, finish it, or remember it at all.

An old, leather-bound volume grabs your attention. You are not sure why you are drawn to it. You open the book and are shocked to see your family name at the top of the first page. Intrigued, you start scanning the book. The subject is your family. Generation by generation, your ancestors tell their story, page after page. The book is filled with remarkable individual stories. They tell of who they were, what they did, the struggles they went through, what was important to them, and the goals and dreams they were trying to achieve. Some were rich, some were poor; they spoke various languages and lived in numerous countries.

But what stands out is that much more than the differences, your family had a remarkable unity and direction, as if all the generations somehow joined together as one team. Their traditions and identity were very important to them. This family didn't just live – they were living for something. They lived beautiful lives, and struggled (and, so far, succeeded) in passing on their traditions generation after generation.

A thought comes into your mind and you momentarily close the book. Can it be? Dare you look? You hesitate and briefly consider returning the book to its place on the shelf and walking away. But you don't. You know there is no choice but to look at the last entry.

It has your name and date of birth. The rest of the page is blank, clearly waiting for you to describe your place in the family saga.

Part of you rejects the implications of this book and wishes you had never opened it. Generations past cannot obligate you to anything. Their ideals were theirs, not yours. They are gone. You are here. No one else can tell you how to lead your life.

But another part of you, the deeper and truer part, knows why you were drawn to this book. In a moment, your life has been changed.

You were not born into a vacuum. You are part of a chain of people who strove for something meaningful and sacrificed for something beautiful. The fulfillment of their lives, hopes and dreams depends on you.

Will you walk away from the book and its implications? Or will you write a chapter of your own and then pass the book onto your children to do their part?[1]

The person in that book-filled room is each and every one of us. The commitment to keep our families Jewish is the commitment to continue a remarkable chain going back through the generations. The dreams and hopes of our ancestors depend on our adding another link to the Jewish chain. This is an awesome responsibility, and an ancient one.

The Jewish people is the oldest nation on earth. After almost four thousand years, we still speak the same language, live the same culture, pray to the same God, and are attached to the same land. Our survival, generation after generation of keeping our families Jewish, is a miracle.

Mark Twain commented:

> If the statistics are right, the Jews constitute but one percent of the human race. It suggests a nebulous dim puff of star dust lost in the blaze of the Milky Way. Properly the Jew ought hardly to be heard of; but he is heard of, has always been heard of. He is as prominent on the planet as any other people, and his commercial importance is extravagantly out of proportion to the smallness of his bulk. His contributions to the world's list of great names in literature, science, art, music, finance, medicine, and abstruse learning are also way out of proportion to the weakness of his numbers. He has made a marvelous fight in this world, in all the ages, and has done it with his hands tied behind him. He could be vain of himself, and be excused for it. The Egyptian, the Babylonian, and the Persian rose, filled the planet with sound and splendor, then faded to dream stuff and passed away; the Greek and the Roman followed, and made a vast noise, and they are gone; other peoples have sprung up and held their torch high for a time, but it burned out, and they sit in twilight now, or have vanished. The Jew saw them all, beat them all, and is now what he always was, exhibiting no decadence, no infirmities of age, no weakening of his parts, no slowing of his energies, no dulling of his alert and aggressive mind. All things are mortal but the Jew; all other forces pass, but he remains. What is the secret of his immortality?[2]

As Jewish parents, we have an opportunity to continue the story, to add a page in our unique book, and to keep the Jewish link strong.

Appreciating the Gift

True, most of us didn't choose to be Jewish, but our heritage is not a burden. Living as Jews is a privilege and a joy. We give our children a precious gift by instilling within them a vibrant Jewish identity.

When life is going well, when we have friends, when we are in a loving relationship, when we have a good job, we can easily forget about God. When people are young – single or newly married—they sometimes ignore religion altogether.

However, people go through hard times. People lose jobs. People have trouble in their relationships. Life is not all roses. Human beings need a religion, a belief system. We long for one. Faith adds immeasurably to our lives and helps us be happy, productive members of society. We have an inner need for purpose and meaning. We have a deep drive to connect to something greater than ourselves.

Why do so many Jews today feel disconnected from their religion? They were given expensive Bar and Bat Mitzvahs but little meaning. Their deepest needs were not met. Some will try to fill these needs with other religions. Some will try to fill these needs with traveling and other endeavors that provide a sense of rising above the mundane. Some will suffer emotionally because they feel the emptiness. But a person needs a religion, needs faith.

And a person needs a community. We have the Internet and cell phones. We are well connected. Yet we don't know what it is to be part of a community. We are surrounded by people but often feel alone. We have many Facebook friends, but how many close ones? We have many teachers, but how many mentors?

Growing up with a Jewish identity is beneficial for children because they acquire a sense of who they are, a sense of comfort and belonging that helps them throughout life. Their Jewish experiences growing up add tremendously to their childhood: Chanukah lights and their timeless message; the Passover Seder and its lessons of history, freedom, and hope; the shofar of Rosh Hashanah; the family togetherness of Friday night dinner. Jewish holidays and life cycle events provide fun times, sweet memories, and valuable lessons for life.

Being part of a Jewish community provides friends, community, solid values and shared ideals for the whole family. The family is not alone, rather we are part of a community, part of a whole, involved in valuable activities and building valuable relationships.

Valuing Diversity

The benefits of belonging are not just for the individual and the family. They extend to the world as a whole.

Our appreciation of multiculturalism is a wonderful improvement over the past. Throughout history, life has not been easy for minorities. They were often discriminated against, persecuted, and even killed because of their differences. Today, in Western countries at least, not only are minorities "tolerated" but their uniqueness is actually valued. A true universal vision of life needs and wants minority subcultures to survive and thrive.

In today's world, people *want* different cultures to exist and value the diversity of contributions made by different cultures. We Jews are also a small minority culture that should survive and thrive. Our culture and way of life has sustained us throughout our remarkable journey for two thousand years. Jewish religion, culture, and life are a rich, multi-colored and ever-vibrant piece of the great human tapestry. It would be a terrible loss for us, and for the world, if our culture and religion faded from view.

Valuing Judaism

Every culture and every heritage has some social and psychological benefits for individuals and families, and many cultures are necessary for a diverse planet. For us, as Jews, our culture and religion offer even more.

When the first Jews, Abraham and Sarah, appeared on the scene almost 4000 years ago, mankind worshipped the stars and the sun. The gods were essentially powerful people who fought battles and won wars, much like the humans who imagined them. Humans fashioned idols, and bowed down to them and sacrificed their children to the gods of fire.

The ancient world was cruel. Ancient Rome and Greece had neither soup kitchens nor public hospitals. Deformed babies were left to die, and the highest form of entertainment was watching human beings be torn to pieces by animals who had been starved purposely to provide a good show.

We, the Jews, were the rebels of the ancient world. Abraham was called the *Ivri*—"Hebrew"—because the word "*Ivri*" means to "cross over." Abraham crossed to the other side of the world in philosophical terms: he challenged the ancient world's views and broke its idols.

We Jews taught the world that every individual is created in the image of God and that human life is sacred. We taught that there is an obligation to help others, not to hurt them, and that each of our lives has purpose and meaning: We are more than merely advanced animals. The ultimate idea we taught is that there is indeed One God, a loving Creator who cares for us, and wants the best for us.

The world has come a long way, and because so many of our ideas have prevailed, we forget where they came from. Yet, the fact is that Jewish life and its ideas and ideals have had a uniquely far-reaching impact on human civilization.

John Adams, second President of the United States, said:

"I will insist that the Hebrews have done more to civilize men than any other nation. If I were an atheist, and believed in blind eternal fate, I should still believe that fate had ordained the Jews to be the most essential instrument for civilizing the nations. If I were an atheist of the other sect, who believe or pretend to believe that all is ordered by chance, I should believe that chance had ordered the Jews to preserve and propagate to all mankind the doctrine of a supreme, intelligent, wise, almighty sovereign of the universe, which I believe to be the great essential principle of all morality, and consequently of all civilization."[3]

(Non-Jewish) historian Paul Johnson put it this way:

"Certainly, the world without the Jews would have been a radically different place ... To them we owe the idea of equality before the law, both divine and human; of the sanctity of life and the dignity of human person; of the individual conscience and so a personal redemption; of collective conscience and so of social responsibility; of peace as an abstract ideal and love as the foundation of justice, and many other items which constitute the basic moral furniture of the human mind. Without Jews it might have been a much emptier place."[4]

We are indeed a special people, with a unique role in history. The world is an emptier place when anyone loses touch with his or her culture and traditions. In light of our astonishing contributions and role in the world, there is an extra dose of sadness when the person is Jewish.

What Parents Want

Thankfully, the Jewish link does not need to disappear. As parents, we want to enjoy our children, share fun times, and create sweet memories. We also want to raise good children with a strong sense of who they are, sharing good values with a positive peer-group.

Despite high assimilation rates, most Jewish parents also want their children to be proud Jews, to love their heritage, and to stay Jewish. We may not be clear ourselves what this means, we may not do too much about it, but being Jewish means something to us. Deep down, we feel that being Jewish is something worth holding on to, worth the effort to be lovingly passed to the next generation.

So what can typical Jewish American parents do? What should you focus on? What works and what doesn't? Is education the answer? Holidays? Youth groups? Visits to Israel? What if parents aren't particularly knowledgeable or committed?

What Does the research Show?

Over the last fifteen years, I have done extensive research, conducted countless interviews, attended conferences, and been in ongoing contact with Jewish families around the world. I have also been busy raising my own Jewish family. What I offer in this book are not my own suggestions, but rather a summary of facts as they exist – what the literature, research, and anecdotal evidence indicate that parents should do to keep their families Jewish. No one individual element is enough or will overcome all obstacles – only a combination of factors will produce significant results. Ideally, both parents will work together in encouraging their family's Jewish pride. But if you are a single parent, or if your spouse is not presently interested or able to be your partner in this journey, you can still have a major impact on your child's Jewish identity.

The title of this book was carefully chosen. There is one overall goal and method that is the key to unlocking other doors to Jewish identity and continuity: a positive, warm, loving and happy Jewish environment. If you want to keep your family Jewish, you must create this type of environment for your family, and this book is for you. In it, we will explore together the role of parents, the types of activities to introduce, the best forms of Jewish education, and discuss becoming part of a community. Each section will explain the issue as a broad principle and then offer specific suggestions to help put theory into practice. The best way to benefit from this book is to read it through in its entirety once, in order to best understand the challenges and opportunities that await Jewish parents. After this first read, parents can return to sections and suggestions that seem most appropriate for their lives right now.

PART 1:

Parents

Many intelligent and successful Jewish people feel nervous when it comes to the "Jewish" part of parenting. While Jewish parenting requires effort on your part, the good news is that you probably know more than you think you do about raising Jewish children. The rest can be easily learned and put into practice.

The first part of this book establishes what your role is as a Jewish parent, what type of home environment you can create, and what support you will need. You will be able to choose a few small, easy steps that will enable you to be a more effective Jewish parent.

CHAPTER 1

Practice Joyful Judaism

Your attitude towards being Jewish has a large impact on your children's attitudes towards being Jewish. You must find ways to make Judaism joyful in your own life and in the lives of your family. In order to begin to understand why this is so, consider the following story about the Cuban Missile Crisis:

The year is 1962. John F. Kennedy was President of the United States. At the height of the Cold War, Cuba had been taken over by Fidel Castro and aligned itself with the Soviet Union.

The Russians were building nuclear weapons launchers in Cuba, which is only 90 miles away from the coast of Florida. The missiles could wipe out Washington, DC and a large part of the USA. JFK decided to stand up to the Communists. For almost three weeks, the situation was very tense. American citizens were told that if the Russians launch their weapons, there would be a 16 minute warning before—the end.

Thank God, the Russians backed down and dismantled the missile installations. Everything ended well.

A few weeks after the Cuban missile crisis ended, there was an Alcoholics Anonymous meeting somewhere on the East Coast. At the meeting, a regular participant, Tim, was smiling. He had been sober for over 12 years and joked: "If I only had a few minutes left to live – boy would I have a drink!"

People chuckled and the meeting went on. Still, Tim had revealed something about himself.

Tim had accomplished a tremendous amount and deserves our utmost respect. He battled his alcoholism and stayed sober for

12 years. That took strength, devotion, and discipline. Whatever his motivating factors were – to save his marriage, his family, job, health, sanity, or something else – he stood up to a disease and won.

And yet, when he thought of only having a short time left to live, what did Tim think of? Hugging his wife? Holding his children? Watching the sunset?

No, he thought of drinking. With only a few minutes left in life to do something meaningful or enjoyable, he thought of alcohol.

Tim was still an addict. He kept sober because he had to, but when he thought of something to make him happy, something with meaning, he forgot all about his wife and family and thought of drinking.

He had worked very hard to keep sober for years, but he didn't enjoy the sober life. He stayed sober out of obligation, not enjoyment.[5]

Many Jews in the world today feel a loyalty to Judaism. They belong to synagogues and/or Jewish Community Centers. They give money to Israel. They try to keep some Jewish traditions. They put effort into being good Jews and hope their children will do the same.

However, if you were to ask these people what they enjoy in life, they'll tell you that they enjoy movies, sports, dancing, music, travel and good food. Rarely will they mention anything Jewish. Their Jewish identity is certainly a part of their lives, a serious part. But it is like Tim's connection to sobriety—an obligation: "I stay Jewish because I need to. It is the right thing to do. Staying Jewish is important, but being Jewish doesn't make me happy. It doesn't bring me joy."

The Yom Kippur Syndrome

Yom Kippur, the Day of Atonement, is the holiest day of the year. Yom Kippur is a beautiful day, an invigorating day, but for most people it is also a serious and solemn day—a day of prayer and, traditionally, fasting.

14

How many Jews keep Yom Kippur in some form? According to the National Jewish Population survey of 2001, 59 percent of Jews fast on Yom Kippur. Many others commemorate the fast in other ways.[6]

Yom Kippur lasts for one day and its theme is repentance. Five days after Yom Kippur is a holiday called Sukkot, which lasts for eight days. What is the theme of Sukkot? Repentance? Sin? Fasting? No. Its central theme is joy! The Torah says about Sukkot: "You should be joyous in your celebration of the festival."[7]

Sukkot is an entire week devoted to joy—friends, family, community, beautiful ideas, eating, drinking, and music. Yet how many Jews observe Sukkot in any way?

Sadly the answer is very few. In fact, while the High Holidays (Rosh Hashanahh and Yom Kippur), Passover and Hanukah are the subjects of much research, NJPS and other surveys don't even bother surveying Sukkot observance. Our festival of joy doesn't even make it on the radar screen of communal research.

Think about the perspective this gives rise to. Most Jews look at Judaism with Yom Kippur glasses – seeing Judaism as serious, solemn, and anything but joyful.

While Jews definitely have obligations and responsibilities, we are meant to live happy—even joyous—lives. In ancient Israel, one of the highlights of the year was during the holiday of Sukkot. The Talmud states that whoever did not see this rejoicing, "never saw a celebration."[8]

Being joyous is a theme that runs throughout our tradition. The great medieval scholar Maimonides wrote, "Be consistently in a happy mood."[9] The Bible itself instructed, "You shall rejoice with all the good that the Almighty has given you."[10]

In Hebrew, the word "mitzvah" refers to both a commandment and a good deed. Chassidic Master Rabbi Nachman of Breslov is famous for saying, "It is a great mitzvah to be constantly joyous!"[11]

Does all this sound like a solemn, serious, boring religion?

Judaism is a religion and culture predicated on a healthy balance of joy and responsibility. Yet far too many Jews live their whole lives as Jews without actually enjoying their Jewishness. Their Judaism is one of obligation, not enjoyment.

In the long term, this "unbalanced" Jewish identity can't work as a sustaining force for Jewish identity.

People don't walk away from Judaism because it is captivating, exciting, and fun. People leave because they feel that Judaism is old, boring, and disconnected from their lives. The converse is also true: enjoying our Jewish lives will help keep generations Jewish.

A Lesson for Parents

In terms of parenting, living life as a "loyal but unhappy about it" Jew is a recipe for disaster.

As human beings we go to great efforts to do what we find enjoyable and avoid activities that we don't enjoy. We "forget" to take out the garbage, "put off" losing weight for later, "don't get around to" paying the bills. In essence, we find ways of avoiding what we don't enjoy doing.

If Judaism is unpleasant, children will do what they are forced to, usually until they are teenagers. Then they will run away from Jewish activities and do what is more pleasant.

If we want our children to "stay Jewish" we need to help them enjoy being Jewish.[12] If children enjoy being Jewish, then everything else in this book becomes much easier. How can parents make sure that their children enjoy being Jewish?

Work on Being Happier

To a large extent, happy parents produce happy children. There are of course exceptions, but I am often surprised by how strong the rule is. As Rabbi Nachman of Breslov explained, "When you are happy, you are able to cheer up other people, which is a great act of kindness. A happy person spreads his positive feelings." [13]

How can we be happier? A full answer requires a whole book, but here are two simple ideas that usually help:

Firstly, learn to be more grateful. Each day notice one new thing to be thankful for. This adds up quickly. In a small amount of time, you'll realize how much we all have to be grateful for. The more people appreciate what they have, the more positive their attitude will be. Suddenly, the hassles, disappointments and frustrations of daily life seem less problematic. They don't disappear, but they are less overwhelming.

Second, think happy thoughts. At first, you may have to force yourself[14] to do this, but the effort is worth it. Over time, this "artificial" thinking becomes more and more natural and our state of being changes for the positive.

By making yourself happier, you are very likely to make your children happier. The happier your children are, the more likely they are to enjoy the family traditions and activities that come along with being Jewish.

Enjoy Your Judaism More

If parents enjoy the Jewish holidays and life cycle events, there is a much greater chance that their children will as well. If parents feel that Judaism is a burden, their children are more likely to run away from their heritage.

Some Jewish immigrants to America at the beginning of the 20th Century would complain about their difficult lives, *"S'iz shver tzu zein a Yid—it's difficult to be a Jew."* This attitude, while understandable then, will not inspire our children to remain Jewish.

Parents need to be enthusiastic about being Jewish. Our attitude toward Jewish activities should be one of joy and happiness. After all, Judaism is here to *add* to our lives, not make them harder! As Rabbi Nosson Tzvi Finkel, head of the great Slobodka yeshiva explained, "The commandments were given for our ultimate happiness and pleasure. The goal of …the Torah is to give a person a way of living that will greatly enhance his life."[15]

Have Fun With the Children

Sing, dance, joke around, and smile. If you are the serious type, stop being so serious all the time! Children need fun and laughs and giggles and smiles.

If the children *enjoy* being with you – rather than just spend time with you when they have no choice – your influence over them is enormous. They'll be in a positive mood and also enthusiastically join you in the "Jewish stuff." Their minds will be open and positive to your example.

Engage in Fun Jewish Activities

Many families make the mistake of forcing Judaism on their children. This usually doesn't work. The children will listen now, but with resentment. They'll run away at the first chance.

Being Jewish is a joy and a privilege, and should be lived that way. If the children hate going to synagogue and feel forced to do so, parents are not sowing the seeds of a committed Jewish adult. Rather, they are setting themselves up for failure. Of course we want our children to come to synagogue, make Jewish friends and become familiar with Jewish prayer and rituals. But we need to find ways to help them enjoy Synagogue.

Celebration of the weekly Sabbath is a wonderful component of Jewish life. In my family, sitting at the Shabbat table is a privilege, not an obligation. Between the delicious food, special desserts, singing, stories, powerful lessons about life, and extra attention from the parents, *most* of the children want to be there, *most* of the time. That is fine. We want them to enjoy Shabbat, not feel chained by it.

One mother I know had a wonderful idea. When she lights the Shabbat candles on Friday afternoon before sunset, she gives each child a big hug and kiss – and a lollipop! Can you imagine what kind of subconscious effect that has? Are you surprised that her children look forward to Shabbat and enjoy candle-lighting?

In many families, for each major holiday, children receive something new—a toy, new clothing, or other gift—and on Passover night, they receive their best present of the year. In these homes, Jewishness is automatically associated with special and happy times.

Use The Holidays

The Jewish holidays are great opportunities to make being Jewish exciting and fun. If your children are in day school, they'll be taught all about the holidays and be looking forward to them. If your children are in public school, pull them out of school to celebrate Jewish holidays. They appreciate the change, and the holidays are a wonderful opportunity for family time, singing, great food, interesting stories, and lots of fun.[16]

Final Thoughts

With a little work, parents can make the atmosphere of their homes happier. With a little insight and planning, Jewish parents can – and need to – make their family's connection to Judaism a happy and positive one.

GETTING PRACTICAL

The more a person enjoys being Jewish, the more likely they are to remain Jewish. Therefore:

- Make sure your home is a happy home

- Smile, sing, and dance

- Find ways to enjoy Judaism more yourself – it will affect everyone else

- Engage in fun Jewish activities

- Celebrate "happy" holidays such as Purim, Sukkot, and Simchat Torah

- Help your children make Jewish friends to enjoy Jewish activities more

CHAPTER 2

Be a Role Model

Parents are children's first and (usually) most influential teachers. As a parent, you have a uniquely pivotal role to play, often in ways that will surprise you. The next story about Diane Sawyer teaches a fascinating lesson about influencing people:

I remember a powerful <u>60 Minutes</u> discussion in the midst of the 1984 re-election campaign of then President Ronald Reagan. Diane Sawyer, one of the show's hosts, revealed an illuminating experience that resulted from a previous segment on the campaign. Her first report was a long, critical analysis of Reagan's first term in office.

Viewers saw pictures of the President visiting a homeless shelter, while her voice dubbed over the images explained that in fact he had cut money to such institutions and the numbers of poor had skyrocketed during his tenure.

Viewers saw Reagan glad-handing with African-Americans while she described his attacks on affirmative action and other programs dear to the African-American community.

Viewers saw Reagan with schoolchildren and heard Sawyer rail against his massive cuts in school funding.

Viewers saw Reagan at the stock exchange while she quoted economics and finance experts attacking his policies.

Her report continued for eight minutes (a lifetime in television terms) and by the end of it, the honesty, credibility, and reputation of the White House had suffered, she felt, serious damage.

She was sure that the Reagan Administration would be so incensed that she feared that her White House press pass would be revoked.

After the show, Sawyer was quite surprised when the White House press secretary called to <u>thank her</u> for her segment.

"I spent eight minutes on prime time television attacking you! Why are you thanking me?" she asked.

"Diane," he replied, "I'm surprised at you. You are one of the best, most respected journalists in the world today and you still don't understand. No one listens to the news. People watch the news. We call it tele<u>vision </u>and they are viewers. You gave us eight minutes of golden images. We couldn't have paid for better."

The lesson was clear: we are a *visual* society, and what we *say* is often only of secondary importance.

This story is especially relevant in raising children: if we want our children to grow up with the inner feeling that being Jewish is important and central to their identities, *they have to see us engaged in Jewish activities.* These include reading Jewish books, lighting candles, listening to Jewish music, watching Jewish videos, writing a check to support Israel and other Jewish causes, going to a weekly class, attending synagogue, and much more.

Whatever the activity is, if the children don't see it, it isn't real.

What children see affects them. In our quest to be role models, we must not simply "talk the talk" but also "walk the walk."

Pride on the Outside

A few weeks after Senator Joe Lieberman was chosen to be presidential candidate Al Gore's running mate in 2000, I received the following message. I'm not sure who wrote the e-mail, but it had obviously been forwarded dozens of times and presumably had been read by many thousands of Jews around the world.

When you read the e-mail, don't focus on whether or not you like or agree with Joe Lieberman. Try and focus on the message of the writer.

I never thought that in my lifetime I would see an observant Jew on a major party presidential ticket. I emphasize the word "observant." There are, and have been, any number of Jews elected to governmental positions on the national, state, and local levels. In fact, presently 11 of the 100 U.S. Senators are Jewish. Most come from states with minimal Jewish populations-Oregon, Wisconsin (both senators are Jewish), Minnesota, Connecticut, and Michigan-and, of course, the states with a large Jewish presence-New York, California (both senators are Jewish), New Jersey, and Pennsylvania. With all due respect to these senators, and the many other elected Jewish officials, only Senator Joe Lieberman demonstrates on a daily basis a commitment to the mitzvoth (commandments) of Jewish life. In the past few days, the entire country has been introduced to what it means to be an "observant" Jew. The television has shown Sen. Joseph Lieberman kissing the mezuzah on his doorpost as he left his home to greet the press. America has been told that Joe Lieberman does not campaign on Shabbat or Jewish holidays, he doesn't write or use electricity on Shabbat, but he still casts votes on Shabbat since it is done to promote "the respect and protection of human life and well-being."

From the standpoint of Jewish education, we couldn't ask for a better American role model for our youngsters. Senator Lieberman demonstrates that it's not "uncool" to be openly observant and Jewish. His example teaches that Jewish principles are not limited to the synagogue, but have an important role to play even in the White House.

The Jewish world was enthralled by Joe Lieberman. Most Jews were proud that a Jew made it (almost) "to the top." But this was more than just ethnic/religious identification at work. Many Jews admired that Lieberman was obviously proud of being Jewish!

Unlike many others who relegate their Judaism to the sidelines, to him being Jewish was center stage, and defined his being.

Compare this to a nice Jewish fellow who is proud to be Jewish, but does nothing Jewish. Or a person who says, "I have a Jewish heart." Who will have a bigger effect on their children's identity?

Remember, what we see is real to us. What we don't see – even if it is "in the heart" – is less real, and much less likely to affect us. Children will be inspired about Jewish identity when they *see* us engaged in Jewish activities.

Meet the Friedmans

Imagine the following scenario. David and Joanne Friedman realize that they should do more to try and solidify their children's Jewish identity. Here's what they do:

- They send their children to Jewish summer camps.
- The next time they move, they choose to live in an area with lots of Jews.
- They encourage their older children to visit Israel.

The Friedmans have taken some significant steps and understandably feel quite happy with these decisions.

But as they get older, the children begin to notice something about their family's Jewish focus. All the parents' involvement with Judaism is focused on the children. On their own, the parents never discuss anything Jewish or invest any time in it. They show no particular interest in going to Israel, learning more about Judaism, or being more active members of a synagogue.

Despite their talk about the importance of being Jewish, and their admirable decisions regarding the children, the parents are sending a very clear message: "We want *you* children to be involved Jewishly. But we adults don't do this stuff because it is irrelevant for grown-ups."

Relevance

Children need to see that Jewishness is not just for children. When children see their parents "doing Jewish", they intuit that being Jewish is a key part of life. Judaism is not just for children, but rather has relevance throughout life.

This idea of relevance is a fundamental aspect of human nature. Usually, people will only invest their time and energy into activities they believe will help them in life. Singer and songwriter Shaun Murphy was once asked what advice she would give young people, and she answered, "I'll always regret not continuing with those piano lessons my mother tried to give me, [saying] 'What did she know? I'm never going to need this stuff' ..." [17]

Most teenagers will accept tasks that they themselves understand to be important. This is why most children don't drop out of school. They understand that graduating from high school is imperative in life.

But if children – especially teenagers—feel that they are being asked to waste time on activities that don't have any relation to their future lives, they will resist investing time and effort into those subjects. Adolescents begin to resist *children's stuff* [18] as part of their struggle for independence.

What is the best way that parents can show that being Jewish is relevant throughout life, and isn't just for children? By being active themselves.

If we want our children to take their Hebrew and Jewish studies seriously, they must see that being Jewish is a significant part of adult life – not just classes for children. The best way for children to grasp this is if they see their parents using and valuing Jewish knowledge and practice. If children don't connect Jewish knowledge and life with being adults, they will regard it as something to be avoided at all costs, put up with when necessary, and discarded as soon as possible – usually right after Bar or Bat Mitzvah.

Is Synagogue Membership Enough?

Being an active member of a Jewish community and a synagogue is crucial to our families' Jewish identities. However, simply being a member without being active is not enough.

Consider the findings of Dr. Bruce Phillips's often-quoted study on Jewish family life:

"Simply paying dues for synagogue membership, or financially supporting Jewish causes – in other words, a checkbook commitment to Judaism, without a personal commitment of time and energy – makes no impression whatsoever on children." [19]

According to rabbis, cantors, lay leaders, and synagogue members I have met with in Jewish communities around the world, many if not *most* people join synagogues today to obtain seats for the High Holidays, ensure their children a Bar or Bat Mitzvah, and secure a place to be buried.

Those are the top three motivating factors. People who join for these reasons are hardly active in the synagogue at all. They pay their dues, give the children the Bar and Bat Mitzvah, and tell themselves (and their children!) that "we've done our duty."

This approach is weak because parents are usually the central Jewish role models in their children's lives. As researcher Dr. Mark Rosen put it:

"Children, especially young children, emulate their parents. The role that parents play in the home cannot be duplicated by any outside

Jewish institution, educator, or program. Parents have far more contact with their children than Jewish educators. If what is learned outside the home is not modeled and reinforced in the home, it is less likely to be sustained ... Parents transmit Jewish identity. For better or worse, parents unquestionably are a major influence on children's Jewish identities and the Jewish future."[20]

When children see their parents showing little interest in Jewish life, they get the message that Jewish identity is secondary, at best. They usually end up showing little interest in staying Jewish.

All or Nothing?

Is Judaism all or nothing? No, and neither is Jewish parenting.

The key is to be a serious Jew, not a perfect one.

If people think that Judaism is all or nothing, most will respond with an honest realization that they are unwilling to do everything and so they end up doing nothing.

We don't need to be perfect. However, we do need to realize that children can be brutally honest. They notice seeming hypocrisy and aren't afraid to point out our inconsistencies. How should we react?

For example, how should parents respond when a child asks, "Why do we keep kosher in the house but eat in non-kosher restaurants?" or "Why do we go to synagogue on Saturday mornings but not Friday nights?"

Some parents will feel flustered, guilty, or defensive when challenged in this way. A good approach is to simply explain that Judaism is about learning and growing in our Jewish identities. Being Jewish is about moving in a positive direction.

Human beings are neither perfect nor perfectly consistent. We live and grow and go through processes. Keeping some practices even though a person is presently unwilling to do 'everything' is not hypocrisy – it is a positive step in the right direction.

What Jewish Activities?

We've seen that parents need to be active role models. We've also seen that life is a process, and we can't expect people to do everything tomorrow.

So what should parents do? Where does one start?

The key is to start doing *something* Jewish as soon as possible. The steps suggested here are small and easy. Choose what appeals to you most and get started. Specifics are far less critical than kick-starting your Jewish momentum.

Some parents simply turn their Sunday night family dinner into a Friday night family dinner and don't answer the phone during the meal. Over time they will learn to say the beautiful blessings that are traditionally said and incorporate other rituals into their Shabbat celebration.

Others start buying Jewish books – for children and adults—and reading them. Judaica stores have thousands of titles to choose from.

Some families decide they will only bring Kosher meat into the house, even if they are not ready to go fully kosher yet. Others start going to synagogue once a week, either on Saturday morning or Friday night. Many plan a trip to Israel and arrange for some Jewish learning while they are there.

There are few rules to choosing a starting point – only meaning, enjoyment, and a great example for your children.

One Hour, Once a Week

If you're looking for something enjoyable and interesting that will make an enormous impact on you and your children, try attending a Torah class for one hour, once a week. This Jewish learning can be as part of a home study group, at a synagogue or adult education center, or elsewhere.

I am often asked the same question by parents. This is how the conversation goes:

PARENTS: "I really want my children to identify as Jews. And I'm concerned – they have no Jewish connections and little interest. What do I do?"

ME: [I then give my standard 4-5 specific suggestions and continue] "... furthermore, I would suggest to you that it is important that you devote one hour a week to learning Torah. "

PARENTS: "What?! How can I possibly get my children to learn Torah once a week?! I told you they aren't interested right now and didn't like Hebrew school..."

ME: "No," I explain. "I wasn't talking about them. I mean for you to learn Torah once a week." You decide what to study, etc. If you need help, I'll give you ideas and find you someone to study with."

More often than not, when I make this recommendation, parents tell me, "We have no problems with Judaism. We're too busy to learn Torah every week. We are just concerned about our children!"

Why is it important for parents to study Judaism once a week?

Here is the actual text of an e-mail I sent to a Jewish father in New Jersey who was very concerned about his children's lack of Jewish identity:

----- Original Message -----
From: "Doron Kornbluth" <info@doronkornbluth.com>
To:—>

Sent: Monday, July 17, 2006 11:37 AM

Subject: Re: response to questions in your e-mail

... On a final note, I humbly suggest that you begin attending a weekly Torah class. I have a lot of connections all over so I can easily help you find something if you want.

Why?

First, because, your children need to see that as people go through life, they start to care more about religion. This is crucial and you are their main example.

Second, they need to see how central your Jewish identity is to you and how it will always affect your relationship with them.

Third, you need to be stronger, more knowledgeable, and confident about the importance of Judaism and Jewish knowledge, etc. Your children's issues about their Jewish identity will likely not solve themselves in a day, week or month and the stronger you are the more likely you will be to see them through to a successful conclusion.

Fourth, I'm not the mystical type but will share one slightly mystical idea. Family units are critical. If one link in the family is moving away, sometimes another link – for example, one or both of the parents—can become a little stronger in their Judaism and bring him or her back. I know it sounds spooky, but I have seen too many cases where it works to omit mentioning it.

Fifth, from what you've told me, you are highly educated in many, many areas, yet haven't opened a Jewish book since your Bar Mitzvah. You have the right (responsibility?!) to be knowledgeable about being Jewish as well.

Finally, you'll enjoy it tremendously. You can choose from many subjects of interest and join millions and millions of satisfied customers.

Warm regards and keep me in the loop.

DK

People who have never delved into Jewish texts are sometimes surprised how enjoyable Jewish study is. But it is.

Jewish Content

For many years, some Jewish organizations were virtually Judaism-free. They felt that Jewish cultural activities, Israeli folk dancing, Holocaust education and pro-Israel rallies were enough to keep Jews Jewish. Even for many synagogues, adult Jewish education was low on the list of priorities. Rabbis who did want to emphasize adult Jewish education because of all their other responsibilities had little time for teaching adults Torah, and little demand from parents themselves.

But the situation has changed. With the startling rates of assimilation in most of the Jewish world today, Jewish communities around the globe have woken up to the fact that a key to Jewish *contin*uity is Jewish *content*. In other words, knowledge and study of Judaism are important because when people learn Torah, even for just one hour a week, the chances that their children will identify as Jews increase dramatically.

Too Old?

It is never too late to begin Jewish education, and Jewish study can add much to life, wherever in life you are. Consider the story of Rabbi Akiva, who lived in Israel almost two thousand years ago. He was an illiterate shepherd until he was forty years old. One day, he saw a hole that flowing water had cut into a rock and his life changed. He realized that if something as insignificant as a trickle of water could affect solid stone, certainly Torah could affect him. With his wife's support, he learned the aleph-bet and applied himself to Jewish learning for many years. Eventually, he became one of the greatest Torah scholars in our history.

Give Priority to Jewish Activities

Some families make a clear distinction between the Jewish and non-Jewish activities their children are involved in. The children know that when something is Jewish or promotes Jewish identity, the parents will invest time and money to make it happen. These children hear responses like these:

- "Jewish youth group program for me to drive you to? Yes! When and where?"
- "Money for Jewish books? Yes! How much?"
- "Sleep over at Jewish summer camp reunion? Yes! When will you be home?"

For non-Jewish activities, however, the parents are not as quick to agree.

Aside from the added Jewish activities that these children are experiencing, they are receiving a valuable message as well: They know what their parents' priorities are. They know that Jewish identity is at the top of the list, and the parents are willing to put time and money behind their words. What better example could there be?

In the same vein, intermarried parents whose children are Jewish should be mindful of the visual impression their very marriage gives about their priorities. Even when Jewish identity is present in the home, the message children receive is confusing. If being Jewish is important and one should make efforts to keep the heritage alive, why did Mommy marry Daddy? Can this really be so vital when it isn't vital at all to one of my parents? Or both? There are certainly children of intermarriage who grow up as strongly identified Jews, but they are a small minority.[21] Parents in this situation must make extra efforts to strengthen their children's Jewish identities.

Final Thoughts

The heart of good parenting is being a personal example. Even if parents only follow some of the specific suggestions mentioned in this book, but are passionate about Judaism and demonstrate through their own actions that Judaism is a top priority for them, children will often follow suit.

On the other hand, if parents do not involve themselves Jewishly in a serious way, but rather, adopt a shallow program to "raise Jewish children," children will see right through the enterprise and rebel. To one degree or another, many Jewish families today are caught in this trap.

Relying on the personal example of parents alone is quite risky, however. While parents have much more influence on their children than they realize, they are far from the only pull. Without Jewish friends, schools, camps, and activities, children will naturally gravitate toward non-Jewish peers and influences. If parents are loving and supportive, their children's natural desire to please them and win their approval will go a long way, but it is unwise to rely on that alone.

When parents invest in helping their children feel more Jewish through the methods suggested in this book *and* act as strong role models, then children are receiving one clear message. The education and inspiration they are receiving from their parents, their activities, and their environment all emphasize how wonderful Jewish identity is.

GETTING PRACTICAL

Actions speak louder than words. Therefore:

- Get involved in the Jewish community

- Be a Jewish role model

- Do more than you do presently. Judaism is not all or nothing.

- Devote one hour a week to Jewish learning

- Show your priorities by investing time and money into your family's Jewish life

CHAPTER 3

Create a Jewish Home

The Diane Sawyer story recounted in the previous chapter has another implication: Our homes should look like Jewish homes.

As Rabbi Dovid Orlofsky writes:

The things we use to decorate our children's rooms — and for that matter, our own homes — impress our children with what we value. ... A fellow I knew once asked to meet with me to discuss his children. Although he wasn't observant, it was very important to him that his children marry Jewish people. While we were talking he told me about his late grandfather, who had been a Talmudic scholar. His grandfather had left him crates of Jewish books. The man told me that since they were in Hebrew he had no use for them and I was free to take what I wanted. I refused. "Those books are your inheritance," I told him. "If you're worried about who your children are going to marry, then take those books out of the garage and display them in your living room. Let your children see that they're more important to you than valuable antiques or china."[22]

In combination with other strategies outlined in this book, making a home look more Jewish can have a significant conscious and subconscious effect on the children growing up in it. If we want them to know that we value Judaism, let them *see* us value our tradition in the home. For, as Rabbi Benjamin Blech writes in *The Complete Idiot's Guide to Understanding Judaism*, "We visit the synagogue. We live in our homes…Judaism believes that the most central house of God is not the synagogue but the home."[23]

Let's now get practical: how can parents make their home look more Jewish? Here are some basic ways to do so, but don't let these examples limit you—use your imagination!

Mezuzah

A *mezuzah* is a sign to our visitors and to ourselves that this home is a Jewish one. Furthermore, by putting up a mezuzah, we remind ourselves of the God who commanded us to do so, and connect ourselves to millions of Jews around the world who do the same.

The nice *mezuzah* covers commonly found fulfill two roles. They are protective, to safeguard the *mezuzah* from harm, and decorative, as it is appropriate to make commandments as beautiful as possible.

The main ingredient in a *mezuzah* is the parchment. The scroll contains passages from Deuteronomy 6:4-9 and 11:13-21, written by a scribe. Beginning with the famous Shema prayer, *"Hear, O Israel: The Lord Our God, The Lord is One,"* the parchment also includes the verses that command us to put "these words" upon our doorposts, which are the Scriptural source for mezuzahs.

Traditionally, a mezuzah is often understood to act as special protection from harm. Maimonides explains the mezuzah as a reminder of God's presence.[24] Whether their function is mystical, educational or both, a Jewish home declares itself as such with a mezuzah.

Mizrach

Did you know that all synagogues around the world face Jerusalem? The Talmud explains that if we are outside of Israel, we should face Israel to pray. If we are in Israel, we should face

Jerusalem. If we are already in Jerusalem, we face the Temple area. If we are at the Western Wall, we should face the holiest part of the ancient Temple that stood above.

Jerusalem is the capital of the Jewish homeland and the Jewish people. The Western Wall area is what Judaism considers the holiest place on the planet. By praying in its direction, we show solidarity and unity with all our fellow Jews around the world who also face Jerusalem to pray today, and throughout history.

In order to always know which direction to face in prayer, we need to know where Jerusalem is. Custom arose in western countries to place a small sign on the eastern wall of the house—the direction of Jerusalem. These reminders are often quite beautiful, and can be painted, embroidered, or use any other art form. They usually have the word "mizrach," east, written on them, and thus have become known as "mizrachs." Practically speaking, while Jews in New York and Calcutta will both be facing Jerusalem, one will be facing east while the other will be facing west. Wherever you are, a mizrach is a beautiful Jewish ornament that not only identifies the house as Jewish but also reminds us of Jerusalem and Israel.

Jewish Paintings

Growing up, my grandparents had a painting on the wall of Ruth and Naomi from the story in the Book of Ruth. The painting was rarely a subject of conversation, but its being on the walls made an impression nonetheless. I knew they had the painting on the walls because they were Jewish.

At a deeper level, displaying Jewish art around is a subconscious reminder that Judaism is not just about books and prayers. Our identity as Jews should permeate all we do, even our appreciation of art.

What is Jewish art?

Many people enjoy pictures of Israel, stories from the Bible, famous Jewish personages, European Jewish towns and Chassidim dancing. However, the definition of Jewish art is much wider. For our purposes, let us define Jewish art as anything that emphasizes our connection to the Jewish people, the Jewish land, Jewish history, or Judaism itself.

In recent times the range of good Jewish art has become just about as large as the range of good art. Subjects are varied and styles include modern, abstract, impressionist, cubist, realist, and more—something for every taste.

Ketubah

A Ketubah is the traditional Jewish wedding document. Ketubahs are so central to Jewish marriage that grooms have been handing their brides beautifully decorated ones at least since medieval times.[25]

In our day, many couples hang beautiful Ketubahs on the walls of their homes, symbolizing the strength of their marriage and their desire for their relationship to be based on Jewish values and ideals. If you don't have one from your wedding, it is never too late to choose a Ketubah you like (printed or custom made) and proudly display it.

Other Jewish Art

Jewish paintings and Ketubahs add Jewish flavor to the home and emphasize to all present the feeling that being Jewish is an important part of our lives. But don't stop there.

Why not add in some Jewish content to your display cabinet? Proudly display your Shabbat candlesticks, Kiddush Cup, Chanukah Menorah, various kippot, china dreidels, a Shofar,

Jewish crafts the children have made, items you brought back from Israel, a pretty *Havdalah* set, and so on.

Also consider a framed traditional blessing on the home, called a "Birchat HaBayit." Similarly, a lawyer can display the verse "Justice, justice, you shall pursue"[26] and a doctor can display Maimonides' prayer for healers. Many options exist and most are available at your local Judaica store or online.

Hebrew and Jewish Books

The Jewish love affair with Jewish books has been well documented throughout the ages by both Jews and non-Jews. Here are some examples of what has been said about the subject.

"Cover your bookcases with rugs or linens of fine quality; preserve them from dampness and mice and injury; for it is your books that are your true treasure."

MEDIEVAL SCHOLAR IBN TIBBON

"To an extent unequalled among other sections of humanity, Jews have been interested in books... (The Jew) copied books. He owned books. He patronized literature. He was interested in intellectual life and... movements. Even in the most soul-destroying periods of oppression, it might be assumed that almost every ghetto Jew, however humble his circumstances and however lowly his calling, was likely to have his modest library. A book was not to him, as to his neighbor, an object of veneration, of mystery, of distrust. It was a sheer necessity of everyday life."[27]

HISTORIAN CECIL ROTH

While the main purpose of Jewish books is to be read and studied, just having them around can be valuable as well. Their presence sends a clear message that not only is being Jewish a central part of this home, but being knowledgeable about Judaism is also important. Whether or not you read Hebrew, your home should have on its shelves some basic Hebrew (or Hebrew-English) books such as a prayerbook (siddur), copy of the Torah (Chumash), Passover Haggadot, and High Holiday prayer books. These send the unstated message to your children that the Jewish religion and Hebrew language are important to you as well.

Are you embarrassed that you can't read them? Simply explain to your children, "I wish I could read them, but at least I have them. I hope someday we'll read them together."

Jewish Photographs

Which pictures do you have up in your home? The beautiful sunset in Hawaii or the sunrise at Masada in Israel? Is it the children's graduation pictures or their Bar/Bat Mitzvah pictures?

The pictures that people choose to put up in their home often indicate what they value the most.

Let your favorite shot of the Western Wall be displayed to show your connection to Israel. Let proud family photos indicate your strong connection to your roots. Display photos of your children in Jewish settings and at Jewish occasions to emphasize which activities and milestones touch you the most: first day of Jewish school, Jewish camp, Bar or Bat Mitzvah, youth group, Israel. Show pride at their Jewish accomplishments and look forward to the next events.

Other Visuals

Jewish art is not the only way to make an impression. Jewish antiques and old coins are available. You'll find opportunities for Jewish visuals all around the house. For example, the refrigerator door is a great place for magnetic Hebrew letters.

Consider buying a Jewish calendar for your kitchen. Why? Most American calendars today have the High Holidays printed on them, which is wonderful, but they still remain American calendars with a few Jewish holidays stuck in. A Jewish calendar has all the same information, along with pictures, artwork, etc.—and all with a Jewish theme.

Jewish-themed key chains, cookbooks, games, a Hebrew letter chart, toys, jewelry, Jewish and Israeli newspapers, baby bibs, t-shirts, etc., all add to the impression that being Jewish is a part of life. Other people have returned from Israel with sandals, clothes, facial creams, or water pitchers, in order to "bring a little Israel" home with them. A friend had a lamp with a statue of Moses holding the Ten Commandments. This may not be your taste, but you get the idea.

Furthermore, visuals outside the home are noteworthy as well. For example, taking children to a joyous Jewish wedding can leave a big impression. Witnessing a solidarity rally for Israel and other similar activities can also have a long-term effect. The principle is that children are affected by what they see.

Final Thoughts

Your home is central to developing your children's Jewish identity. Home is where they spend most of their time and where they learn about life. By displaying outward signs of your Jewish identity, you are also showing that being Jewish is one of the main parts of your life.

GETTING PRACTICAL

Your home should look like a Jewish home. Therefore:

- Put Mezuzahs on the doorposts

- Buy Jewish and Israeli art and photographs

- Display your Ketubah (wedding document) in a prominent place

- Include Jewish artifacts in your display cabinet

- Buy, read, and display Jewish and Hebrew books

- Place a Jewish calendar on your refrigerator

CHAPTER 4

Seek Support and Guidance

At certain times in life it is imperative to stand with one's principles and be willing to "go it alone" for the sake of what is right.

That being said, in day-to-day life, it is extremely difficult, if not impossible, to always "be the loner." Most of us need support from our surroundings. I learned this lesson well when I first arrived in Israel. I wanted to fit in and so tried speaking only in Hebrew and spending all of my time with native Israelis.

Eventually, although my new-found friends were very nice, I realized that this isolation from English-speakers had gone too far. Living in a new country is difficult enough—being alone in one's struggles makes the adjustment all the more difficult.

This is true in all of life. Human beings are social animals. We like to be around other people, and, more than that, we like to be around similarly-minded people. Sometimes we need to be different and stand out. But in the long term, being alone is not easy.

Parents who want to strengthen their family's Jewish identity should seek out some friends who feel the same way. Like-minded friends can make the goal of strengthening Jewish pride much easier – and more pleasurable – to attain. They can share experiences and ideas. They can help you reflect on your family's particular issues.

Without like-minded friends, you risk feeling alone in your goal, making Jewish continuity seem (and be) much more difficult. Over the long-term, this will both hamper your efforts to keep your family Jewish and weaken your resolve to follow-through.

This doesn't mean that you should ignore non-Jewish friends or Jewish friends who are not particularly interested in their Jewish identity. However, it is very helpful to try and develop new friendships in order to give yourself support as well as share practical information about good Jewish school programs, after-school activities, good books to read, holiday recipes, and more.

If you are part of a group of like-minded parents, you'll be able to gain perspective and advice on dealing with many of life's issues from a Jewish family perspective. Furthermore, usually children will be more open to a new activity or behavior (a Friday night dinner, for example) more when they see other parents doing it. If they feel that their family is the only one doing something, they may object. But if their friends' families do the same thing, they'll usually go along much more happily. Making connections to other involved Jewish families makes the whole process smoother and easier.

Where can a family find like-minded families? The best places to find active Jewish families are in places such families frequent: Synagogues, Jewish schools, Jewish Community Centers (JCCs) and other Jewish organizations.

The Synagogue

Joining a synagogue is crucial in order to get the support and guidance families need to keep their Jewish identity strong.

When choosing a synagogue, keep in mind that you should be active members, not just an address on a mailing list. Getting involved will help you meet many people who also care about their children's Jewish identities. While no single synagogue is likely to fill all your Jewish needs, the environment should be a positive and comfortable one for you and your family.

Many factors need to be considered in choosing a synagogue. Does the synagogue have families you identify with? Are their children of the same age as yours? Are you impressed by their behavior? Is the synagogue small enough to meet people? Do you find the services enjoyable and inspirational? Is there an adult education program that you can benefit from? Are the adults committed to Jewish learning and growth?

The real goal is to be part of a thriving community. Look for ways to get involved. For example, one parent who was a talented speaker offered to help Bar and Bat Mitzvah candidates with their Hebrew lessons and speech. One parent drove the youth group to social outings. Other parents would help with synagogue cookouts. The goal is to meet other Jewish families and become an active member of the community.

Finding a Rabbi

Many people think of a Rabbi as a religious functionary whose central role is to officiate at weddings, perform funerals, give sermons, and make sure the prayer service is performed correctly. While rabbis do indeed fulfill these tasks, any learned layperson can do them as well. These functions are not why we need rabbis.

Furthermore, Jewish spiritual leaders do not function as intermediaries between us and God. Judaism does not believe in such intermediaries—each and every one of us can access God. This is also not the reason we need rabbis.

So what *is* the role of the rabbi? Let us begin by looking at the origin of the role of the rabbi. Moses was the first rabbi of the

Jewish People—the Chief Rabbi, so to speak. What was his main role? To this day he is called *Moshe Rabbeinu,* which is translated as "Moses our Teacher." The primary role of a rabbi has always been to teach us about our heritage and inspire us to improve ourselves as people and as Jews. In addition to this, a rabbi serves as a guidance and marriage counselor, a social worker, an official clergy performing weddings and funerals, and much more. In order to be successful, a rabbi must have the personality to match. A rabbi must be humble, pleasant, and honest. Furthermore, a rabbi must certainly have deep knowledge of Judaism, including the written Torah (Five Books of Moses), the Talmud, and more recent works. This knowledge is the beginning, but not the end. In Judaism, rabbis do not sit alone on mountain tops or enter monasteries. They get married, have families, and deal with life issues. They can thus better help *us* deal with life issues. That is one of their main functions.

Not every rabbi will be right for you and your family. Unfortunately, some people have had negative experiences with individual rabbis. Despite this, each of us needs to find a rabbi – to develop a relationship of trust and guidance. Having the guidance of a rabbi can help parents make the right Jewish choices for their family. Rabbis are usually good sounding boards and counselors. Without a rabbi, a person can only progress so far.

Real Jewish commitment requires a teacher and guide to help you through the rough spots. For example, what happens when a teenager wants to go to the big game on Yom Kippur night? Your rabbi can help you with that. Ideally, the rabbi should get to know you and your family over the years, being a resource and inspiration as you and your children grow into your heritage.

Sometimes, the rabbi of the synagogue you choose will be the right guide for you. However, many families today are involved with more than one organization and have a choice of rabbis to connect to. Whatever your situation, here are some questions to ask yourself as you look for an appropriate rabbi:

- Is the rabbi knowledgeable and sincere?
- Is the rabbi a good teacher?
- Do I respect this person? Do my children feel the same way?
- Is this person's family life something I admire?
- Is this person accessible, relatable, and non-judgmental?

Final Thoughts

Forging a relationship with a rabbi or teacher has many benefits. You will gain insights into Jewish life and philosophy. You will benefit from experienced guidance on crucial life issues. You will also send an important message to your children, namely that Jewish people should be in touch with our teachers and leaders. When your children go to college and are faced with difficult decisions, they are more likely to form a connection with a rabbi there as well.

GETTING PRACTICAL

Keeping your family Jewish is much easier if you have support and guidance. Therefore:

- Join a synagogue

- Get involved in the Jewish community

- Forge a connection with rabbi and/or teacher

- Make efforts to maintain friendships with like-minded Jewish families

PART 2
Children

Because you make the decisions when the children are young and living at home, providing a Jewish environment for holidays, life cycle events and other activities in the early years is easier. Soon enough, however, children grow up and leave home. Your goal as a Jewish parent should be that your children's Jewish feelings are sufficiently developed to keep them Jewish once they live on their own.

This part of the book will explain how Jewish feelings develop and how parents can encourage their children to be involved in their own Jewish identities. It includes many practical suggestions regarding the Jewish holidays, life cycle events, and daily life. Finally, because much of Jewish identity is based on the religion of Judaism, you will learn how to talk to your children about God.

CHAPTER 5

Get Children Active

Your actions and attitudes as a Jewish parent are key, but only part of the picture. Children need to be active as well. In order to understand why, read the following story.

It was Czarist Russia and the Russian army loved drafting young Jews – officially 16 years and older but often much younger boys. The draft was specifically designed to take Jews away from Jewish life and assimilate them, and their "term of service" was no less than 25 years.

A local Jewish boy had just been 'recruited' off the main street of the village. The new rabbi in town was told that the Russian commander had hinted that for the right price, the boy could be freed. The problem was that he demanded three thousand rubles – an exorbitant sum.

"Is there anyone in this area that has that kind of money?" asked the new rabbi.

There was someone, the rabbi was told. But it was Old Yaakov, an old miser who lived alone in a huge house and never gave a cent of charity.

The rabbi went straight to Yaakov's house and knocked on the door.

"I don't give money if that is what you are here for," said a voice from inside.

"I would just like to sit down and talk with you. Won't you please let me in?" responded the Rabbi.

Old Yaakov opened the door. The rabbi and the miser sat together on a couch. Soon, they were speaking like old friends. Laughing and sometimes weeping, they talked for hours.

The rabbi then got up and said, "I had a strong feeling that we should meet. I am glad we did. I must go now, but please visit me soon."

The miser had tears in his eyes. He escorted the rabbi to the door. "Rabbi..."

"Yes?"

"Thank you for coming and spending so much time with me. Rabbi, I know there must have been some reason you came. What is it?"

The Rabbi explained the situation and the miser, with great pain on his face, reached into his pocket and handed over 50 kopecks – quite a paltry sum.

The Rabbi warmly took the money and began praising the miser and thanking him for helping free the boy. The miser then gave another few rubles and the Rabbi increased his praises accordingly.

The Rabbi then got into the carriage and waved goodbye. The miser ran up to the door and said, "Rabbi – how much do you need?" The Rabbi responded and within a few minutes, the miser was back with a sack full of coins.

"There it is, Rabbi. That is all you need. Go and save the boy. And thank you for redeeming me as well."

This time the Rabbi was silent. He looked at the miser in the eyes, nodded, and motioned to the driver to move on.

All is well that ends well, especially in a story. He rode home, paid the commander, and saved the boy.

Later, the Rabbi explained to his stunned congregants, what happened

"I couldn't sit there and do nothing. It was clear that there was only one person who could help – Yaakov the miser.

Yaakov was an orphan. But no one cared for him or took care of him. He was a young boy and he was alone. He slept in the forest. He carried pails of water to make a little money to survive. It was a terrible, hard life, but he worked hard and eventually he had a roof over his head and food on his table. He was not rich by any means, but no longer homeless and hungry.

One day a beggar came to his door and asked for charity. Yaakov had worked so hard for the money. He had starved for his money.

But he decided to give. So he handed the man 10 kopecks. The beggar looked at the coin, looked at Yaakov and snarled. He threw the coin to the ground. He spit in Yaakov's face. 'Money? You call that money? I need rubles and you give me 10 kopecks!'

Yaakov was destroyed. He had worked so hard to have some money and offered it to someone else in need. He had literally starved to earn those precious kopecks. They were thrown back in his face. He vowed never to give money again. And he didn't.

So I spent time with him, opening his heart. When he gave a little, I praised him enormously, breaking down the walls. Eventually his heart was open and so was his purse."

We can learn many lessons from this fascinating story. In our discussion of Jewish parenting, one lesson stands out.

If a beggar rudely rejected my donation, I'd be upset. I'd blame him. I'd blame myself. The incident would probably ruin my day. But I wouldn't retreat into a hermit-like miserly existence for 20 years! Neither would you.

So why was Yaakov the Miser so deeply affected by the beggar's rejection? Yaakov had worked so hard for his money that he cared much more about it than most of us do. Most of us won't even pick up a dime on the street, let alone a penny. Although we may try to be careful, most of us simply aren't so affected by the loss of a few cents. Yaakov, on the other hand, was deeply hurt by the rejection of his money because he had worked extremely hard to earn it. He cared so much about the money because he had worked so hard to earn it. This is a fundamental principle that will affect our own lives and the lives of our children, and teaches us an important less that we can all learn from.

Do you know what the Hebrew word for love is? *Ahava*. The word *Ahava* comes from the word *Hav*, which literally means "to give." The Hebrew word for love in reality means "giving." Remarkable, isn't it? What are we meant to learn? That loving comes from giving. The people or causes we give the most to are the ones we come to care about, and love, the most.

Save the Whales

Let's take the example of whales. I like whales. I've gone whale-watching and hope to go again some day. They are beautiful, majestic animals. I am glad that various animals' rights groups are working to protect them. But on the list of the most central concerns in my life, how high do they rank, honestly?

Not in the top ten. My family, community, the Jewish People, humanity, are all above whales. Would the whales be in the top 25? I doubt it.

Now let us say that for the next twelve months, I worked day and night for the Save the Whales organization. I wrote letters, read, and wrote articles. I demonstrated. I gave my time, money, energy, and thought. I even risked my life on Greenpeace boats trying to block illegal whale hunting.

Before embarking on my year-of-the-whale, while I certainly admired them, their welfare was low on my personal list of priorities. Would these have changed at the end of the year? How would I feel about the whales then?

A person who spends a year living and breathing for the whales is going to start caring about them a lot more. This occurs because what we give to, we come to care about.

This is why parents care so much about their children—we give so much to them. For a woman this holds true from the moment she learns that she is expecting. Then she goes through the birth itself. From then on, the giving starts for dad as well— the sleepless nights, the diapers, the doctor visits, the crying. Parenting young children can be overwhelming—we *constantly* give to our children. By this time, when the physical giving lessens, we are still giving emotionally—and financially.

Finally we've put them through college and we think our job is done. But they're in their thirties and still asking for money! It never ends. Parents *love* their children so much because they *give* to their children so much.

The Lesson for Parents

From the story of Yaakov the Miser, Jewish parents can learn a fundamental lesson about strengthening our children's Jewish identity.

People care about what *they* invest in, what they build and spend time and energy on. If we want our children to care about their Jewish identities, we need to make sure that they are active in their Jewish lives. Identity can't all come from us.

We need to help our children get involved – meaning investing their time and energy—into Jewish activities. If everything comes from us, and they only passively go along, when they mature into independent young people, their Jewish identities are not likely to be strong. Why? Because all along *we* were the ones being active. Not *them*. Their own feelings about being Jewish never had the proper opportunity to develop.

Final Thoughts

If children become involved themselves, give their time, energy, and thought to Jewish activities and causes, their feelings will naturally grow. The Jewish attachment they have will be *theirs*, not only something coming from their parents. Because the Jewish feelings are theirs, they are much more likely to last.

GETTING PRACTICAL

The more individuals invest their time and energy into something, the more they come to care about it. Therefore:

- Get your children involved in Jewish youth groups and prayer services

- Send your children to educational Jewish summer camps and Israel

- Have them help prepare for Jewish holidays by cooking or preparing holiday activities

- Encourage them to pack toys for poor Jewish children, raise money for victims of terror, and visit sick Jewish children in the hospital

- Encourage them to read books with Jewish lessons

CHAPTER 6

Use the Jewish Holidays and Life Cycle Events

The Jewish holidays are the most common way that Jews connect to Judaism. The holidays are wonderful. They are gifts to children to enjoy and learn from. They are gifts to adults to celebrate and be inspired by. Finally, they are gifts to Jewish parents who want to instill a strong Jewish identity in their children because the Jewish holidays are a fun, appealing and powerful way that a family can connect to each other and connect to their Jewish heritage. Parents should not inflict negative holiday experiences on the family. A little preparation can turn a "boring obligation" into a much beloved family ritual. We can, and need to, make our holidays into experiences that the children will *want* to attend. Celebrating the holidays is also a vital protection against non-Jewish influences. A family that celebrates a fun Purim, Sukkot, and Chanukah will avoid most or all of the problems of Christmas.

Maximize the Impact of the Holidays

Each Jewish holiday has its own wonderful lessons and customs, and the cycle of the holidays as a whole also provides a Jewish feeling to the entire year and a regular connection to the Jewish people. The sum is indeed greater than its parts.

In this chapter, we will briefly look at the major holidays, describing the essence of their major themes, what we do on the holiday, and how Jewish parents can best use the holidays to draw their families closer to Judaism. Please note that we will only cover some aspects of the most commonly celebrated holidays. Consider this chapter a beginning.

Shabbat

Shabbat begins shortly before sunset every Friday afternoon. God created the world in six days, stopped on the seventh, and commanded us to do the same. The word Shabbat literally means "to cease." Alternatively called the Sabbath or Shabbos, on this day Jews around the world (and throughout history) stop their daily activities and focus on family, community and spirituality.

Shabbat is such a powerful ingredient in strengthening Jewish identity that one early Zionist thinker, Ahad Ha-am, famously said that, "More than Israel has kept Shabbat, Shabbat has kept Israel."

While today every culture and religion has some form of a weekly day of rest, Shabbat was a revolutionary concept thousands of years ago. Yet Shabbat is not just a day off, but rather the most enjoyable and highest point of the week, when we join together in celebration, discussion, and prayer.

On Shabbat, we leave our jobs behind and try not to talk about work, pressure, or anything depressing. Shabbat is a time to be happy and relaxed. Spouses spend extra time focusing on each other and parents spend extra time with their children. Family, friends, and neighbors socialize and "catch up."

Some special activities that will help create the "Shabbat feeling" in one's home include wearing nicer clothing than one wears during the week, lighting candles before sunset, saying the beautiful (and short) Kiddush prayer over wine, and having Challah, Shabbat bread, to begin the Friday night meal. Many families who want to slowly introduce Shabbat into the family routine will take a first step of lighting candles, making a special meal, and not answering the phone on Friday night in order to "block out" the outside world and have some beautiful family time. Including some kind of age-appropriate "Jewish Talk" at the table not only teaches children and generates memorable discussions, but unites the family around shared goals and values. For little children, this "Jewish Talk" will often include age-appropriate stories, ethical teachings, and basic questions about Judaism and life. For older children and teenagers, consider adding ethical dilemmas from the Torah portion. With time, you will discover what works best with your family.

Singing on Shabbat is a wonderful addition to the family atmosphere. There are many wonderful Shabbat songs including ones that children love and participate in, and they are easy to learn through CDs or at synagogue. Reading some of the thousands of great Jewish books that have been published in recent years helps promote the sense of peace and calm that many enjoy over Shabbat, as well as adding inspiration. Playing board games also adds to the Shabbat atmosphere and brings a family together. Many parents relax the rules on Shabbat, allowing their children to eat sugary cereals and/or leave their beds unmade. Many families take leisurely walks on Shabbat afternoon. With its candles, spices, and wine, the havdalah ceremony at the end of Shabbat is also a children's favorite.

Special foods to delight parents and children include *challot,* the sweet braided loaves of bread that are available in Jewish communities anywhere or can be made at home (This is a good Thursday or Friday activity for children.) Classic European Sabbath fare includes Gefilte fish, soup with matzoh balls, fish, chicken and more. Sephardic cuisine has its own delights and Kosher cookbooks are easily available that include Mexican, French, Japanese, and other culinary options. What's important is that the food be plentiful and delicious – and that the children receive extra treats on this special day.

Rosh Hashanah

Printed on most American calendars, Rosh Hashanah is, literally, the Jewish "New Year." In areas with large Jewish populations, Jewish employees and students are often expected to take the holiday off from work or school. Occurring in the early autumn, the holiday is meant to help us reflect on the previous year, focus priorities for the next, and bring God back into the picture of our lives. The shofar "wakes us up" from our spiritual and moral slumber, and symbolizes the call to repentance.

Children should see that parents are working on self-improvement and are trying to set goals for the coming year. For children, the main activity of Rosh Hashanah is watching and hearing the blowing of the shofar, the ram's horn, which they love and are fascinated by. In most synagogues (the good ones), as long as they remain silent, children are allowed to come close and watch the shofar blowing.

Parents can easily add to the excitement. Buy a shofar at any Judaica shop and have fun together learning how to blow it. A Google search will help you locate audio samples of Shofar blowing online. Let the children try to make the right sounds –*Tekiah*, a long drawn out shrill; *Shevarim*, short bursts; *Truah*, very short shrills. If you don't have a shofar, you can use any horn or even your hands as you prepare for the holiday. The point is that the children have fun and recognize the different sounds.

The Rosh Hashanah custom called Tashlich is also a fantastic opportunity for children. Tashlich takes place next to a body of water where we symbolically cast our sins into the sea. The custom does not actually remove our sins – that is what regret and repentance are for – but does offer a wonderful visual activity for adults and children to remember. Check your Rosh Hashanah prayer book for the text to be recited, find a body of natural water (lake, stream, pond, and so on), and enjoy the walk.

Special foods on Rosh Hashanah include delicious round raisin challahs, and the exciting *simanim* or "signs" of the evening meals. The prayer book includes numerous *simanim*, with the most famous example being dipping an apple in honey to symbolize the sweet year we wish to have.

Yom Kippur

Ten days after Rosh Hashanah is Yom Kippur, literally the "Day of Atonement," the holiest day of the Jewish year. For adults, Yom Kippur is a day of "afflictions," including the well known prohibitions of eating and drinking. These temporary restrictions help us focus on the spiritual dimensions of life and "rise above" the physical needs and interests that fill our days. We do *teshuva* (repent) for our mistakes and much of the day is spent in prayer. Note that if I wronged a friend or family member, I need to receive their forgiveness—Yom Kippur doesn't fix everything for me. Some are surprised that Yom Kippur is not a sad day. We are able to apologize, own up to our mistakes, be forgiven, and move on!

On Yom Kippur, we wear white clothes to symbolize "coming clean." There is a custom to give charity generously between Rosh Hashanah and Yom Kippur, especially on the day before Yom Kippur. At the beginning of the holiday, the Kol Nidrei prayer is sung to a beautiful enchanting melody passed down through the generations. The prayer has taken on a large place in the hearts of the Jewish people.

Children should see parents apologizing to each other and resolving to improve. Although they don't fast, children can join in the special meal before the holiday and in the "break-fast" at the conclusion of the holiday. They can also participate in other customs of the day. All children can wear white and *not* wear their leather shoes (another one of the "afflictions"). Depending on their ages and maturity, children can fast for a short amount of time and attend synagogue. They are usually fascinated by the story of the whale in the Book of Jonah, which is read on this day (best for parents and children to read the story before to know the main outline). The shofar is also blown at the end of Yom Kippur, and that is always a favorite. At the end of the fast, in many synagogues, congregants dance and sing happily – a wonderful end to a holy day.

Sukkot

Five days after the solemn day of Yom Kippur is the eight-day long celebration of Sukkot and Simchat Torah. Joy and happiness are such a central part of the holiday that the Torah itself says: "You shall rejoice on your festival"[28] and Jewish communities host special Sukkot celebrations the entire week.

On Sukkot (literally, "booths" or "huts"), we dwell in temporary huts and shake the Four Species (the myrtle branch, esrog, palm branch and willow) to celebrate God's protection of the Jews in the desert after they left Egypt. "Exiling" ourselves temporarily from the comfort of our homes is a fun family adventure and a deep lesson not to be overly attached to material objects.

Sukkot is made for children: They will love building and decorating the Sukkot booths (look online for instructions) and, weather permitting, eating and even sleeping in them. The meals of the holiday are delicious, fun and—if parents prepare stories or questions to ask – quite meaningful. The Four Species is one of the loveliest of all Jewish "rites," where we wave "the fruits of a pleasant tree, and palm branches, and thick leafy boughs, and willows of the brook, and rejoice." [29] The sights and smells easily appeal to children.

The last part of the Sukkot season is a holiday called Simchat Torah, literally "the joy of the Torah." One of the happiest days of the Jewish year, on Simchat Torah we mark the end of the yearly cycle of Torah reading and the beginning of the new cycle. Parents and children joyously sing and dance around the synagogue, circling the *bimah* where the Torah is read. Children often hold flags (a good activity idea is to make them) and toy Torahs. We celebrate the joy of Judaism.

Since Sukkot is also called the "Harvest Festival," many try to eat the foods of the special seven species of the Land of Israel (wheat, barley, date, pomegranate, fig, olive, grapes), as well as decorate the sukkah with them.

Chanukah

In the middle of winter, we light the Menorah for eight nights in what is referred to as the Festival of Lights. Chanukah (sometimes spelled Hanukah) celebrates two events. First, we defeated the Greeks and their sympathizers, who attempted to force the Jews to abandon Judaism. Then, when the fighting was over, we entered the ancient Temple in Jerusalem, the holiest site in Judaism, and found one day's worth of oil. This oil miraculously lasted eight days, giving us time to produce more for the original Menorah of the Temple.

In large part due to the overwhelming presence of Christmas, Chanukah often takes on a new importance for Jewish families.

This importance is often exaggerated: Chanukah alone will not keep our families Jewish, it is one element of a much larger picture. However, if understood correctly, Chanukah can lend itself to this competition because its theme is our desire and self-sacrifice to keep our families Jewish rather than become assimilated into the majority culture.

Children's activities include spinning tops called *dreidels*, lighting *menorahs* (under parents' supervision), and sometimes even making their own. Some families have theme nights, for example, Frying Latke Night, Dreidel World Series, Relatives' Reunion, Crafts Night, Music Night, Kindness Night, and more. Most importantly, the eight nights of Chanukah are ideal as a special family time, when parents come home early, spend extra time with the children, and everyone lights the Menorahs together. Many families give their children gifts on Chanukah.

Special foods on Chanukah are oil-related, in keeping with the miracle, and include fried potato pancakes (*latkes*), and jelly-filled doughnuts.

Purim

Purim is a joyous holiday occurring in the late winter, one month before Passover.

The name Purim, which literally means "lots," refers to the story of the holiday itself. In ancient Persia, the wicked Haman drew lots to decide on which day the Jews would be destroyed. The holiday reminds us how Esther and Mordechai saved the Jewish people from destruction.

The themes of Purim include celebrating our salvation, coming together in unity, and recognizing that God is orchestrating events for our ultimate benefit, even though we don't always understand how.

The day has four main commandments:

- We listen to the Scroll of Esther (*Megillah*) being read in synagogue.
- We distribute money to the poor.
- We make a special Purim feast with family and friends.
- We give food baskets to neighbors and friends.
- We also dress up in costumes and celebrate! In fact, Purim is so happy that it makes the entire Jewish month of Adar into the happiest of the year. The Talmud says: "When Adar arrives, we increase our joy." [30]

Children of all ages love Purim and can be involved in all aspects of its observance. Before the holiday, they can help make the baskets of food and treats, decorate the house, and choose or prepare their costumes. On the holiday they dress up in costumes and deliver the baskets (this is a wonderful way of building a sense of community.) They can hear the *Megillah* and make loud noises with a noisemaker whenever Haman's name is mentioned! And they can join in the meal, dancing and singing. Also, some children and/or communities enact hilarious Purim plays that are not to be missed.

On Purim we eat special triangular filled pastries called *Hamantashchen*, as well as dumplings. The symbolism is that surprises are hidden beyond what is readily visible. Adults also drink more than normal, as part of the spirit of celebration.

Passover

Passover (in Hebrew, *Pesach*) is an eight day holiday that occurs in the Spring. Pesach literally means to "pass over," thus the English name. When the Egyptians refused to let us leave Egypt, God passed over our homes and punished the Egyptians. The holiday celebrates our Exodus from Egypt and is also called the holiday of Matzoth and *Zman Cherutainu*, the time of our freedom.

Passover is the most popular holiday of the Jewish calendar, with over three quarters of American Jews attending a Passover Seder.[31] Some of the reasons for its popularity include its focus on the positive messages of freedom and hope, and the fact that the Seder is family-centered and creates wonderful childhood memories. Furthermore, Passover touches our Jewish hearts, reminding us that we are part of an ancient chain, going all the way back to the Israelites in the desert.

Commemorating our flight from Egypt when there was no time for the bread to rise, the eight days of Passover are famous for the prohibition against eating bread or other leavened products (*chametz*). We eat Matzoh instead. The other well known element of the holiday is the Seder on the first two nights. The Seder is literally the "order" of ceremonies, the traditional telling and reenacting the story of the Exodus from Egypt.

Do not inflict a boring Passover Seder on your children. With a little foresight, Passover can be the Jewish highlight of the year. The entire holiday, and especially the Seder, was created with children in mind.

In the days preceding the holiday, children can help remove any bread products from their rooms, and then enjoy searching the house for any more with candles or a flashlight on the night before the Seder. At the Seder itself, they can lean on their pillows at the table, spill out drops of wine (or grape juice) at the mention of the plagues, and eat matzoh and delicious *charoset*. Many families make or buy fun props for the Seder, such as frogs to throw when they are mentioned in the Haggadah, or blindfolds to put on for the plague of darkness. Young children practice and ask the four questions, getting much attention and praise in the process. The "Afikomen" matzoh is either hidden for the children to find, or the children "steal" it when the parents aren't looking. In either case, they love to receive special presents as a ransom to give the Afikomen back, and thus enable the parents to finish the Seder. Children can and should participate in the reading of the Haggadah. Most parents will encourage their children to take a long nap in the afternoon and eat dinner early so they'll be able to stay up late and fully participate. Fun aside, on Passover night emphasize to your children who we are, where our people come from, how we survived and why we need to remain committed to our heritage.[32]

Because of its unique limited diet, many Passover cookbooks are available with a wealth of Passover cooking ideas. Passover cooking is different, but can and should be delicious. Aside from eating Matzoh, *Matzoh Brie*, and other matzoh-based meals, you can enjoy delicious Passover cakes and cookies (such as mandelbread) as well as all kind of treats and snacks. At the Seder and during the holiday, many enjoy *charoset* made of wine, nuts, apples, and spices.

Shavuot

Seven weeks after the Passover Seders comes Shavuot. The name literally means "weeks," relating to the period of time between the Exodus from Egypt (Passover) and the giving of the Torah (Shavuot).

Passover is the holiday of freedom from Egypt, but what is the point of freedom? Judaism teaches that the goal was to lead lives of meaning and spirituality as found in the Torah, which we received on Shavuot.

On Shavuot, many Jews stay up all night (or part of it) studying Jewish texts together. On the holiday, we read the Ten Commandments because of their centrality to Judaism. At the time of the giving of the Torah, we all "became Jews," and every year at this time we renew our commitment to Judaism. For this reason, the Book of Ruth is read on Shavuot—she was the paradigm of a righteous convert.

Children can also be involved in the custom of decorating homes and synagogues with greenery. This commemorates the harvest festival aspect of the day, and the fact that the giving of the Torah took place on a lush mountain. Children love staying up late to study with their parents on Shavuot night, even for a short amount of time. Some synagogues organize events specifically for parents and children together. In other cases, parents can take their children to synagogue and sit together to study.

A widespread custom is to eat a dairy meal on Shavuot. Many families will make blintzes, cheesecake, and other dairy delicacies.

Other Special Days: *Lag B'Omer, Tisha B'Av,* and *Israeli Independence Day*

Lag B'Omer is literally the thirty-third day of the Omer, a period of time in which we count from Passover (when we left Egypt) to Shavuot (when we received the Torah). Lag Be'Omer represents the end of a period of mourning for the thousands of students of Rabbi Akiva, as well as the *yahrzeit* (anniversary of death) of Rabbi Shimon Bar Yochai, author of the famed Kabbalist work, the Zohar. In Israel and in Jewish communities worldwide, Lag B'Omer is a day of dancing, singing, and picnics. Keep an eye out in your local Jewish newspaper for community bonfires and celebrations for Jewish families.

Tisha b'Av, literally the ninth [day] of [the Hebrew month of] Av, occurs in the heat of the summer and is the saddest day of the Jewish year. Tisha b'Av marks the day the Temple in

Jerusalem was destroyed and commemorates an extended list of other tragedies that have occurred on this fateful day. The day is similar to Yom Kippur in its restrictions and is designed to reflect and bring on feelings of mourning for the lack of spiritual connection in the world today caused by the destruction of the Temple. Jewish summer camps use the day as a powerful and memorable teaching tool, and if your children are at home for the summer, it is recommended to attend synagogue events: Many communities have special programs, prayer services, videos, and lectures on this day.

Israel Independence Day, while not a religious holiday per se, helps strengthen the Jewish identity and connection to Israel of many Diaspora Jews. Because Israel Independence Day occurs in the spring, most Jewish communities have outdoor Israel Independence Day celebrations, including concerts, Israeli food, a parade, games, Jewish and Israeli vendors, and lots of information about what is going on in the Jewish community. The happy, fun atmosphere and the coming together as a community combine to make this day a success for many Jewish families. Shortly before Israel Independence Day is Holocaust Memorial Day, dedicated to remembering and teaching about the destruction of European Jewry. Also occurring in the spring, several weeks later, is Jerusalem Day, celebrating the re-unification of the Holy City and our renewed ability to access the Western Wall.

The Jewish Life Cycle: Bar and Bat Mitzvah

The main life cycle events involving children are the Bar and Bat Mitzvah celebrations.

The vast majority of Jewish youth have a Bar or Bat Mitzvah ceremony.

Not a few of them look something like this:

Lisa N. marked her [Bas Mitzvah] with a Titanic theme party in Pittsburgh, Pa. According to the Associated Press, the ballroom in one of the city's fanciest hotels was transformed into the luxury liner with 12-foot steaming smokestacks at the buffet table, phosphorescent artificial icebergs, crystal candelabras and replicas of the heart-shaped blue-diamond necklace from the movie. The piece de resistance was a gigantic photo, 10 feet above the floor, featuring Lisa's face superimposed over actress Kate Winslet's body in a famous Titanic scene on the prow of the ocean liner. Lisa appeared to have teen heartthrob Leonardo DiCaprio smiling over her shoulder.[33]

While the Titanic example is extreme, the phenomenon of overindulgent Bar and Bat Mitzvah parties is not:

"... Game rooms for the children that rival carnival midways, emcees, Broadway dancers, the occasional drag queen ... even Las Vegas headliners. Natalie Cole did a bar mitzvah on the aircraft carrier Intrepid in October. Her fee: $150,000 for 30 minutes ... And don't forget about the laser-tag games, the wax hand-sculpture vats, [fireworks, commissioned murals of the kid's favorite band] the computer that morphs a boy's image with his girlfriend's to show you what their offspring would look like, the dog-tag-stamping equipment, the music-video studio, and the mobile photo-processing center that allows you to put a guest's picture on everything from mouse pads to a Rice Krispies box..."[34]

Finally, one popular – and very successful—Bar/Bat Mitzvah DJ advertises himself as follows:

"You're going to need a lot longer than six days and six nights to create this party ... Moses may have parted the Red Sea, but he never had to plan a bar or bat mitzvah celebration that would keep his whole congregation kvelling straight through to next Passover. Now that's a miracle ... This is going to be a simcha of historic proportions ...

We'll bring the look and feel of a Hollywood premier party to your celebration ... Your goal is probably the same as ours: Keep everyone dancing. All night ... Your dance floor will runneth over...[35]

The Bar and Bat Mitzvah scene has certainly gotten out of hand. Many parents intuitively understand that this cannot be what a Bar or Bat Mitzvah is supposed to be about. In order to avoid the materialistic "keeping up with the Joneses" culture and to restore meaning to the event, some families choose to have their Bar or Bat Mitzvah celebration as part of a family trip to Israel. Others stay at home but look into ways to limit the ostentation and increase the depth of the celebration. Both methods are worthy. A beginning point is to understand what a Bar / Bat Mitzvah is.

Until the age of Bar/Bat Mitzvah, Judaism considers a child to be a child. Their mitzvoth (performance of commandments and good deeds) do not fully count. The children are essentially in training. After reaching the age of Bar/Bat Mitzvah, the child is considered a young adult. They become (to a certain degree) responsible for their own religious and moral decisions and are regarded as members of the community. This explains the terminology of the event: "Bar" means "son of" and "Bat" means "daughter of," 'the mitzvoth', or commandments. They have reached a new stage of religious maturity, where their actions count.

While a person becomes Bar or Bat Mitzvah with or without any ceremony or party, Jewish custom (with many variations) is to have some kind of public acknowledgement of the transformation from childhood to young adulthood. The change in status is automatic, but the public acknowledgement adds importance to the transition and hopefully inspires the young person to take their Jewish responsibilities more seriously.

For some, the Bar Mitzvah has become an expensive birthday party coinciding with graduation from Hebrew school. The very ceremony that is supposed to mark the beginning of a new phase of Jewish growth and knowledge has thus turned into the end of Jewish education. Ending Jewish education at Bar or Bat Mitzvah is like teaching a child to read and then refusing to give them books![36] Jewish education is not simply Bar Mitzvah preparation. If we present it as such, there is little chance education will continue after the party, and the children won't learn much anyway, because in fact there isn't that much to know for a Bar or Bat Mitzvah ceremony.

The most important thing for parents to do regarding the Bar or Bat Mitzvah is to keep the event in its proper perspective— it is but one piece in a young person's Jewish development. Adolescents—and parents—will often be made to feel that they need to have the kind of ceremony and celebration their friends are having. This may be legitimate, to a degree, and most families will and should have some type of public celebration.

Along the way, though, parents' priorities make an impression. Do parents care more about the floral arrangements or what their child is learning?

What Jewish youth need is a long term Jewish education program, starting as early as possible and extending much beyond Bar or Bat Mitzvah. Reading from the Torah is far less critical than learning Torah. The latter usually keeps the children Jewish while the former rarely does.

When parents speak at the celebration, they should emphasize their desire that their child sees his or her new Jewish responsibilities as what they are – privileges to be cherished—and ask their children to invest special efforts in their ongoing Jewish education.

Attending Jewish Life Cycle Events

Jewish parents are well advised to make extra efforts to bring Jewish children and adolescents to Jewish life cycle events. Attending a Jewish wedding (at least the ceremony) or other Jewish celebrations is often important enough to warrant taking them out of school. Someone who feels the joy of a Jewish wedding will usually want their own Jewish wedding. Someone who witnesses the deep emotions of continuity and belonging at a Brit Milah, for instance, will envision giving their own son one as well. Parents should prepare their children for the event in order that they understand its significance and rituals. Attending such events strengthens children's Jewish knowledge, connection to community, and overall Jewish identity.

Final Thoughts

When most Jewish people think of Judaism, they think of its holidays and life cycle events. Impressions from the High Holidays, Passover, Chanukah and one's Bar or Bat Mitzvah usually play a prominent role in a person's Jewish memory bank. Because they are so central; boring and meaningless holiday and life cycle events should be avoided at all costs. The good news is that with a small amount of planning, these times can become the happy building blocks of a strong, positive Jewish identity.

GETTING PRACTICAL

The Jewish holidays and life cycle events are peak times to build positive Jewish feelings and memories. Therefore:

- Turn Friday night into a warm and positive family Sabbath dinner

- Spend one hour planning how to make each holiday enjoyable and meaningful for the entire family

- Celebrate Sukkot, Purim, Lag B'Omer and other neglected Jewish holidays

- Bring meaning back into Bar and Bat Mitzvah celebrations

- Bring children to Jewish weddings and other celebrations

CHAPTER 7

Bring Jewish Identity Into Daily Life

The Jewish holidays are wonderful opportunities to keep our families connected to our heritage, but what about the rest of the year?

The Greeks and the Oxen

When the Greeks conquered Israel over two thousand years ago – at the time of the Chanukah story—they wanted to destroy Judaism. They didn't want to physically kill all the Jews; they just wanted us to start living as Greeks and believing in the Greek worldview.

The Greeks made several famous decrees attacking the foundations of Judaism. With these decrees in effect, they felt the entire edifice of Judaism would crumble. What were their three main decrees? They outlawed the study of Torah, the celebration of Shabbat, and circumcision.

When considered individually, these decrees are logical. By outlawing the study of Torah, our knowledge of our religion and traditions would quickly fade. The Greeks understood that individual Jews who know more about their heritage will care more and be more committed to it. Furthermore, whenever Jewish communities have focused on Torah learning, they have resisted assimilation quite well. So we understand why the Greeks attacked the study of Torah.

Celebrating Shabbat is at the core of the spiritual life of Jewish family and community. The Shabbat brings Jews together, strengthens our identity and our connection to each other and to God. The weekly celebration of Shabbat declares to the world – and to ourselves – that we are Jewish. So it makes sense that the Greeks attacked Shabbat. Destroy Shabbat and you have struck a blow at a core element of Judaism.

Outlawing circumcision also is not surprising. The Greeks valued the physical form above all else and felt that the human body was perfect just the way it is. Circumcision proclaims that spirituality and meaning override the physical body, and also symbolizes that humans are not perfect and need to transform and improve themselves. Circumcision was a great affront to the Greeks, both physically and philosophically, and made us "different" when they wanted us to be just like them. So we can easily understand why they outlawed circumcision.

All of these edicts – though evil – were quite understandable. They are pillars of Judaism, and attacking them is reasonable. Yet our tradition records[37] that the Greeks made another, fascinating decree.

They decreed that we had to write on the horns of an ox, "You have no part in the God of Israel."

Now this seems like a very strange decree. What were the Greeks doing? It's easy to understand why they focused their attention on Shabbat, Torah, and circumcision, but why were they concerned with an ox?

The answer is that one of the main elements of our heritage that bothered the Greeks was that Judaism is not just reserved for a few days a year. Judaism is not limited to the weekly Shabbat, and even goes beyond prayer and study, as central as they are.

Judaism addresses every area of life and even includes laws about how we treat animals. Judaism and Jewish ethics tell us which parts of the field are ours and which need to be left to the poor. They tell us when we are allowed to work the field and when not. Judaism teaches us how to infuse ethical, moral, and spiritual values into every realm of life. Jewish law includes what we think of today as secular law – proper business arrangements, criminal acts, and much more.

For the Greeks, religion was confined to their temples. For the Jew, religion affects how we live our daily lives – even in agriculture.

The Greeks made the decree about the ox in order to fight one of Judaism's great strengths – that our religion is in essence a way of life and adds guidance and meaning to our daily lives. The Greeks were not stupid. They attacked the ritual pillars of Judaism, and they also tried to take Judaism out of day-to-day living because they understood that that was precisely where Judaism drew much of its strength from.

It is vital that children see that Judaism is not relegated to the synagogue, religious school, or even trips to Israel. Most of the opportunities we have for Jewish activities occur in our homes, on our vacations, in our business dealings, in how we treat neighbors, friends, and even strangers.

Much of what we do every day has a Jewish dimension to it; we just don't realize it. Learning about the Jewish approach to various facets of daily life adds a whole new dimension to our Jewish lives and the Jewish identity of our children. With a little foresight and thought, many activities that we already do can be easily turned into powerful Jewish experiences that help to define and encourage our children's connection to their heritage. Other actions, though new to some families, are easily applied examples of Judaism affecting our daily lives, not just our Saturday mornings in synagogue.

Let us look at some of the ways Jewish wisdom informs and transforms our daily lives.

"Be a Mentsch!"

The Yiddish word *mentsch* literally means a "human being," but it has come to refer to an honorable person, one who cares about others and acts in a kind, responsible manner.

A person who goes out of his or her way to help an elderly lady cross the street is a *mentsch;* a person who yells at her to "hurry up" is definitely not. A person who checks in on a lonely neighbor and provides some companionship to fill their days is a *mentsch;* the one who ignores other peoples' needs is not. A teenager who helps his or her parents around the house, even when not obligated to, is a *mentsch;* one who doesn't is not.

Judaism has always stressed that the ultimate measure of a person is not how much money they earn or how many degrees are on their walls. God measures us by what kind of person we become, not by what we have. Being a *mentsch* is one central factor in the Jewish value system.

When the children behave nicely, compliment them by saying, "What a *mentsch* – good job." If you need to correct something, try saying, "I know that you are a *mentsch*, and a *mentsch* wouldn't act that way." In this way, you've used the time-tested parenting technique of expressing displeasure at an act while showing appreciation to the person, as well as connecting them to a Jewish ideal of being a *mentsch*.

The best way to teach a child to act like a *mentsch* is for parents to act as *mentschin* themselves. Do we put efforts into helping others? Do we easily become angry and upset? Are we kind and considerate?

Tzedakkah

Statistics show that Jews give more per capita to charitable causes than any other ethnic or religious group.[38] We can be proud of this astounding fact. A fascinating starting point in any discussion of Jewish charity is the fact that Jews do not give *charity* at all.

The word *charity* comes from the Latin word for "love," indicating that the concept is something not obligatory but done because we are loving people. The closest Jewish concept is *tzedakkah*, which is derived from the word *tzedek*, meaning justice or righteousness.

The difference in the words charity and tzedakkah reveals a difference in philosophy as well. Jews donate money to people in need and to important causes because it is the right thing to do, not simply when or because they *feel* like it. It is not surprising, then, that statistics show that the more active people are in their Jewish lives, the more they give. Jewish tradition even sets a minimum amount to give—ten percent of our net income after taxes.

Giving *tzedakkah* needs to be a regular part of life, and children will grow up with an appreciation for the importance of *tzedakkah* if they see you giving. Sending a check from the office doesn't have the same educational effect. Furthermore, for part of your allocations, try sitting down with the older children and deciding where that month's *tzedakkah* money should go. By having a say in the destination, children will be more connected to the act itself, and the activity is much more likely to become a part of them. By making this activity a regular, valued part of life, they will learn about its significance.

Children should also be directly involved in the giving of *tzedakkah*. Having a little *tzedakka* box out in a visible and accessible place will emphasize its importance. Let it be a family custom that small change goes there. If the children receive an allowance or monetary gifts, let them grow up giving 10 percent of their own "income" to those with less. As our tradition makes clear, even those who aren't wealthy should help out those who have less than they do. (Note: some parents have their children pay fines for bad behavior and the money goes to charity. This is a mistake. *Tzedakkah* is an obligation and a privilege, not a punishment.)

Even younger children can participate in giving *tzedakkah*. A beautiful and ancient Jewish custom is to put some money in the charity box right before lighting the Shabbat candles late on Friday afternoon. Children can help put the coins in the box while everyone watches.

In the same vein, participate in food distribution to the needy or volunteer at a food shelter. Children can help pack boxes, collect canned goods and do more.

Welcoming Guests

Many Jewish sources encourage hospitality. Perhaps the most famous is in the Torah itself[39], where Abraham and Sarah welcome three passing wayfarers and exert themselves to provide for their guests. Consider two other famous sources:

> Rabbi Elazar would say, "Hospitality is greater than all the sacred offerings put together."
>
> TALMUD[40]

> "Let your doors be open wide."
>
> TALMUD[41]

Hospitality is a wonderful way to get children more involved in their heritage, and a perfect opportunity to let everyone share in the activity. Invite friends and neighbors over to share a Friday night dinner or just to visit. Open your home to friends and acquaintances and consider becoming involved in Jewish youth groups, synagogue events, and exchange programs where you will be able to host people in your home.

Children can help make beds, bring towels, carry bags, arrange the room, prepare a snack or a drink, and so on. Because welcoming guests is people-oriented, this activity is usually a lot of fun too, and children love to be involved. We can teach our children that one of the most central aspects of being hospitable is to be sensitive to a guest's needs. Sometimes they need conversation, sometimes they need privacy. Through occasional visitors, we can impart to our children the Jewish value of caring, helping, and sharing.

Concern for Neighbors

Our tradition teaches us to go to great lengths to avoid disturbing or harming other people. Tradition explains that we are to build railings around a pit on our property to prevent any mishaps. The same holds true for any dangerous object or situation in our times. For example, we are not to put up a faulty ladder on our property lest a visitor climb it and be harmed.

What are modern examples of the concept? Make sure that we don't disturb the neighbors late at night by making loud noises. Ask our guests not to block anyone's parking space or road access. Keep our property clean so it is not an eyesore.

Whatever the particulars, by striving to be caring and considerate neighbors and citizens, and by subtly letting our children know that in doing so we are trying to fulfill Jewish ideals, we are taking big steps in defining for our families what it means to be a Jew in all spheres of life.

Volunteer Jewishly

Volunteering some of your time to help others is a win-win-win situation.

First, the recipient benefits from needed help, attention, and care. Second, those who give usually end up receiving more than the recipient. Givers do something meaningful, and helping another person can turn an average day into a great one. Third, children who see their parents volunteering for Jewish causes receive a clear lesson that the Jewish value of caring affects their parents' time and schedules, and that their parents value their Jewish identities so much they volunteer in a Jewish context.

Do Jewish organizations have enough staff and volunteers? Some Jews believe they do, and they avoid giving their time (and money) to Jewish causes and instead focus on non-Jewish organizations. In fact, Dr. Sylvia Barak-Fishman's research has shown that "statistically Jews today are much more likely to work for nonsectarian causes than for Jewish causes." [42] This is unfortunate since many important Jewish causes need our help and are desperately lacking for volunteers, organizers, members, and activists. If we Jews don't help our own needy people and causes, who will?

Many opportunities for Jewish volunteering exist. For example:

- Helping in a seniors' home or center
- Visiting seniors privately to cheer them up and give them someone to talk to
- Helping organize or staff synagogue events or youth group activities
- Collecting and distributing food to the Jewish needy (often the elderly or immigrants)
- Visiting the sick or homebound
- Reading stories to younger children in the library
- Mentoring or being a Jewish Big Brother or Sister

When you volunteer in a Jewish context, not only do you teach your children that helping others is important, but you also send a powerful message that "charity begins at home" and that *this*—my Jewishness—is my home.

Pets and Other Animals

Emphasize to your children that compassion for all of God's creatures is a Jewish trait that has been passed down through the ages. Judaism forbids causing any living creature unnecessary pain or anguish in any form whatsoever. We don't believe in hunting for sport, for example, because the taking of animal life is permitted *only* for human need, such as for food or self-protection.

If you have pets, make sure your children know that they need to feed the animals before they eat, as our tradition requires.[43] Teaching your child to treat animals according to Jewish teachings can be a wonderful way of bringing Judaism into daily life.

Say Goodnight Jewishly

Most parents would agree that one of the best moments of the day is when their children go to sleep. True, the quiet is welcome, but bedtime is also special because of the moments of tenderness and affection that often go along with it.

Jewish parents have a wonderful opportunity to put bedtimes into a Jewish context by saying (or, often, singing) the short *Shema* prayer with their children as the little ones close their eyes and go to sleep:

Shema Yisroel, Ado-nai Elo-hainu, Ado-nai Echad.

Hear, O Israel, the Lord is our God, the Lord is One[44].

The *Shema* prayer is the most famous—and the most central— prayer in our tradition and its words encapsulate our belief that there is one God who cares about us and is involved in our lives.

As Dr. Lisa Aiken writes, "the *Shema* literally accompanies us from cradle to grave."[45]

The *Shema* is written on the *mezuzah*, recited at a circumcision ceremony, said in daily prayer services, and was on the lips of Jewish martyrs throughout the ages right before they were killed. The black box from the tragic El Al cargo flight that crashed in Amsterdam in 1992 revealed that the last words of the Israeli pilots was indeed the *Shema*, the ultimate Jewish declaration of faith.

The *Shema* is also the last prayer we say before going to sleep, demonstrating our commitment to fundamental Jewish beliefs at the end of our long hectic days. Jewish tradition encourages children also to say the *Shema* as they go to sleep. The short *Shema* prayer can be taught to them as soon as they learn to speak.

Saying the *Shema* with your children is more than just a touching moment, it can leave powerful, deeply felt Jewish memories, as the following story attests:

[In Europe] during World War II, countless Jewish parents gave their precious children to Christian neighbors and orphanages in the hope that the latter would provide safe havens for them...

In May 1945, Rabbi Eliezer Silver from the United States and Dayan Grunfeld from England were sent as chaplains to liberate some of the death camps. While there, they were told that many Jewish children had been placed in a monastery in Alsace-Lorraine. The rabbis went there to reclaim them. When they approached the priest in charge, they asked that the Jewish children be released into the rabbis' care. "I'm sorry," the priest responded, "but there is no way of knowing which children came here from Jewish families. You must have documentation if you wish me to do what you ask."

Of course, the kind of documentation that the priest wanted was unobtainable at the end of the war. The rabbis asked to see the list of names of children who were in the monastery. As the rabbis read the list, they pointed to those that belonged to Jewish children. "I'm sorry," the priest insisted, "but the names that you pointed to could be either Jewish or Gentile. Miller is a German name, and Markovich is a Russian name, and Swersky is a Polish name. You can't prove that these are Jewish children. If you can't prove which children are Jewish, and do it very quickly, you will have to leave."

One of the rabbis had a brilliant idea. "We'd like to come back again this evening when you are putting the children to sleep." The priest reluctantly agreed. That evening the rabbis came to the dormitory, where row upon row of little beds were arranged. The children, many of whom had been in the monastery since the war started in 1939, were going to sleep. The rabbis walked through the aisles of beds, calling out, "Shema Yisrael—Hear, Israel, the Lord is our God, the Lord is One!" One by one, children burst into tears and shrieked, "Mommy!" "Maman!" "Momma!" "Mamushka!" in each of their native tongues.

The priest had succeeded in teaching these precious Jewish souls about the Trinity, the New Testament, and the Christian savior. Each child knew how to say Mass. But the priest did not succeed in erasing these children's memories of their Jewish mothers — now murdered— putting them to bed every night with the Shema on their lips.[46]

Final Thoughts

Rosh Hashanah is a two day holiday. Yom Kippur lasts for one, Sukkot is seven and Simchat Torah two. Chanukah is eight, Purim is one, Passover is eight, and Shavuot is two. Add in some of the minor holidays and the weekly Shabbat and the grand total is about 90 "special days" a year. This means that even if you celebrate every Shabbat and all the holidays, the remaining 275 days still have nothing particularly Jewish about them. That is a large chunk of time (over 75 per cent of the year!) and it is vital that your children feel Jewish during these days as well. Through the methods suggested here, your children can have a strong Jewish identity whatever the day might be.

GETTING PRACTICAL

For Jewish identity to be meaningful, it needs to be part of regular daily life. Therefore:

- Encourage your child to be a *"mentsch"*

- Give tzedakah (charity) to Jewish causes

- Volunteer for Jewish organizations

- Say goodnight Jewishly

- Show interest in Jewish and Israeli news

- Buy and use Jewish board games

CHAPTER 8

Teach Children About God and Prayer

I f you feel uncomfortable talking with your children about God and prayer, this chapter is for you.[47] Let us start with a story:

Zion National Park in southern Utah is a valley quite hidden from view. From a dry desert landscape above, the access road slowly takes you lower and lower. The view is magnificent – mountains, valleys, waterfalls, lush vegetation. I drove around the perimeter road for a short while and then decided that I would hike up one of the small mountains in the middle of the Park in order to enjoy a good view.

The hike wasn't long. I made it to the top in about an hour and a half at a leisurely, enjoyable pace. When I reached the top, I stopped and took a long drink of water. As I was drinking I opened my eyes and suddenly the world stopped.

It was beautiful beyond belief, and way beyond my expectations. I was awestruck. While I think I only stood there for a few moments, it felt like hours.

I was broken out of my reverie by two noisy teenagers running up the path. Upon reaching the top, they high-fived each other, did a Touchdown dance, and checked their watches.

"24 minutes 35 seconds. Cool. Wanna stay up here and look around? Supposed to be nice," said the first.

"Nah – who cares? Bunch of mountains and trees. Let's go back to the lodge and go online."

"Right," said his friend.

My heart dropped. I felt like a place of worship had been desecrated.

Life is full of wonder. But will we wonder? Elizabeth Barrett Browning wrote:

> Earth's crammed with heaven,
> And every common bush afire with God;
> But only he who sees, takes off his shoes,
> The rest sit around it and pluck blackberries.[48]

In a similar vein, Albert Einstein once said: "There are two ways of looking at the world -- either you see nothing as a miracle or you see everything as a miracle."

People with a healthy sense of wonder have an easier time connecting to religion. A sense of wonder, a sense of humility before the Infinite, a "poetic corner of the soul" – all these bring a person closer to God and Judaism.

Someone with a limited connection to the meta-physical will have a harder time relating to God, praying to God, and connecting to the deepest parts of themselves. As Jewish parents, part of our job is to cultivate our children's sense of wonder.

Children naturally have a sense of wonder, of spirituality, an openness to God, and a belief in the miraculous. However, they still have questions:

- "Why doesn't God just make Grandpa better?"
- "Is God a boy or a girl?"
- "If I talk to God, why doesn't God talk to me?"
- "If God is everywhere, does He watch me in the bathroom?"

Our children will ask us many questions like these. How will we respond? Will we encourage their exploration? Will we change the subject? Will our discomfort be so obvious that they don't ask us again?

The reality is that many Jews are uncomfortable talking about God in a meaningful way. The (non-Jewish) philosopher Blaise Pascal made a famous distinction between the "God of Abraham,

Isaac and Jacob" and the "God of the philosophers." The latter is impersonal, uninterested and doesn't listen to mortal man. Accepting the existence of such a God is relatively easy because little is expected of the believer.

The God that we believe in, however, is the "Living God" Who created the human being "in His own image," spoke to Moses face to face, revealed Himself in the desert, and desperately wants each and every one of us to open our hearts to Him. To talk about such a God is harder. It becomes personal. It has implications. No wonder many people avoid even thinking about God.

While understandable, this is unfortunate for two reasons. First, developing a personal connection to God is one of the main goals of Judaism, and second, the belief in a personal God is so central to Judaism that de-emphasizing God will affects a person's entire Jewish identity.

We want our children to develop a relationship with God and connect to prayer. Having such a relationship is an extraordinary boost to one's self-esteem. Children are not dependent on their friends' approval if they know that God loves them and personally created them in the Divine Image. When times are hard and they feel alone, they know that there is "Someone" listening to them, a "Friend" who is always with them and watching out for them.

Finally, having a familiarity and openness to God's presence makes all of Judaism (prayer, Jewish philosophy and mysticism, text study) less foreign – a big boost for Jewish identity. If we take God out of our children's Jewish lives, we make them strangers to much of our tradition, observances and holidays.

As Jewish parents, we want our children to strongly identify with Judaism and have a place in their heart for God. How can we help them keep their sense of wonder and maintain their openness to the Infinite?

Here are some suggestions that have worked for other parents.

Develop Your Sense of Wonder

Let yourself be in awe of waves crashing, the flames of the Shabbat candles burning, the beauty of a spider web, the roar of thunder, or the peace of an empty beach. The physical world is a wonderful place to connect to the Divine. The more you develop this side of yourself, the better the chances that it will rub off on your children. Look for times and places when you and your children can share in moments of wonder. A walk in the woods or under a starry sky; noticing the sunset out of your window or stopping to take in the beauty of a flower. When you and your children *do* have these special moments, make sure to be open about what you saw and felt. This sharing will deepen your connection to the wonders of life.

Work on Your Own Relationship with God

If children are to develop a relationship with God, parents need to openly be developing one as well. We don't have to be perfect, have all the answers, or erase our doubts. We just need to be working on a relationship. Let your children see you praying. Encourage them to pray as well.

Teach Children that God is Their Greatest Friend

God is with them when they are happy and when they are sad. He wants the best for them. Sometimes God will help them succeed and sometimes He will be with them when they fail, but He always wants the best for them. Be specific. Children learn better through concrete examples than abstract concepts. For example, "God made the sun and moon and stars—and you!" is better than "God makes everything."

Tell Them God Loves Them

When I tell my children that I love them, I often ask them who else loves them. By now, they know that the list includes my wife, grandparents, and God. Make this a constant refrain.

Teach Your Children to Pray

Teach children the "official" prayers and encourage them to make personal requests and prayers in their own words and language. Take them to synagogue where they will see adults praying. If adults take prayer seriously, children will be inspired to do the same. When possible, find a good youth program so they can learn the prayers and see other children praying as well. The first element of teaching and modeling prayer is to have a positive attitude toward it. Let yourself see prayer as a privilege, not a burden. Try to look forward to prayer instead of looking forward to its conclusion. Parents who develop within themselves a positive attitude such as this are more likely to have children who see prayer the same way.

Talk About God

Children have a natural openness to God's existence. Let them ask any and all questions about God, belief, and prayer. Don't be offended if they challenge you. Children and teenagers often test out ideas they do not fully believe in. Your negative or harsh reactions may do more to determine their actual beliefs than the original statements they made. Be thankful that they are discussing the subject with you.

How can you answer their questions? Begin making a list of common questions and answers about God and prayer. Here are a few examples of the kinds of questions that children may ask:

"Doesn't God know what I need?" "Why do I need to pray?" "Why pray out loud?" "Why not say whatever words I feel like?" "Why do bad things happen to good people?" These are all excellent questions, whether they come from adults or children. How would you answer these questions? Do you have anything intelligent to say?

When you can't answer a question, say, "That is a great question. I don't know but let us find out together." Then find out. This approach has many benefits: It shows the child that you take their questions seriously; it answers their questions; and it shows that we don't have to have all the answers, as long as we are willing to learn.

Final Thoughts

By opening ourselves to the wonder of life and the possibility of a relationship with God, we enrich our own lives and the lives of those around us. By helping our children nurture a sense of wonder and opening their minds and hearts to prayer, we are enabling them to connect to Judaism at a level of awe, humility, and depth rather than obligation.

GETTING PRACTICAL

God and prayer are central to the Jewish tradition. For children to feel connected to Judaism, they should be exposed to Jewish spirituality. Therefore:

• Develop and help your children develop a sense of wonder and connection to God

• Teach children that God loves them

• Teach children to pray

PART 3
Education

One of the greatest determinants of a person's long-term Jewish commitment is their Jewish education. Simply put, the more a young person knows about being Jewish, the more likely he or she is to remain strongly Jewish as they mature. As parents, we need to think carefully about the kind of Jewish education we are going to give our children because the ramifications of this decision will echo for years, even generations, to come.

This section will offer crucial information about the primary decisions you are likely to face: when Jewish education should begin, how long it should last, and of what type it should be. Included in the discussion will be the core question of Jewish day schools, as well as early childhood Jewish education, other youth programs, and vital considerations for the college years.

CHAPTER 9

Choose a Jewish Preschool

P roviding our children with a strong Jewish education starts early, with preschool, includes many programs for Jewish youth, and continues into the college years. Let us consider each of these in turn.

Early Childhood Education[49]

Jewish ECE (Early Childhood Education) programs exist around the country, with approximately 125, 000 students[50] and are an important first step in building a child's Jewish identity. The Jewish tradition has much to say about children from birth until age 2 or 2.5. Jewish infant care, Mommy & Me, and other programs can help new parents learn timeless parenting principles and share core Jewish values. These early years are the brain's fastest growing time and the environment should be supportive, helping to "hard wire" a child's mind to associate with Jewish activities with pleasure.

Early environment and relationships in the first years of a child's life are essential to determining what kind of person the child will become.[51] Young children are like sponges, soaking up knowledge, and they are shaped by these formative experiences for life. For example, people that are not exposed to different languages and accents in their early years have a much more difficult time learning to speak a second language. Early environments and exposures *do* matter.

As the Talmud puts it:

"What is learned in early childhood is absorbed in the blood."[52]

Parents choose Jewish ECE programs for many reasons. Some want the Jewish content while others want the high quality and convenience, and see the Jewish environment as no more than a bonus. [53]

Regardless of their original reasons for choosing a Jewish preschool, parents are impressed with the education, values, and Jewish connections: Approximately 90 percent of all parents report being "very satisfied" with both the school as a whole and with the Jewish content in particular.[54]

Jewish preschools have many benefits:

- High quality Early Childhood Education and child care
- A warm, loving environment with professional teachers who care about the children
- Positive Jewish associations and memories from the beginning of the education process
- For the parents: meeting other Jewish parents in similar stages of life[55]
- For the family: Jewish inspiration and a gateway into the Jewish community

Good Jewish preschools focus on Jewish values such as peace, respect, community, family, honesty, study, and self-discipline. These schools are places where your children will learn and experience activities based on the values that you want your children to learn. Your child will learn to give charity on Friday mornings, visit old age homes, care for animals and the environment, and learn what it means to be a *mentsch*. Teachers will introduce children to the Jewish holidays, teach them basic Hebrew words and some Shabbat songs, and bake challah with them every Friday.

While a high quality Jewish preschool will endeavor to instill Jewish identity and Jewish values, please note that not all Jewish preschools are equal. Some have a minimal Jewish connection and almost no Jewish content. Many of these have significant numbers of non-Jewish personnel and non-Jewish families. Some do not even have "Jewish" in their mission statement. While they may or may not be good schools, they will not build the child's Jewish identity – a great opportunity lost.

For a growing number of Jewish parents and preschools, Jewish ECE is a solid first step in a strong Jewish education and one important component of the overall picture of Jewish involvement. Preschools bring families together and solidify Jewish values. They instill a positive, happy Jewish identity so that the home and school can reinforce each other.

Consider these comments from parents of Jewish preschool children:

"I did a lot of research before we decided where to send our daughter. Turns out the Jewish preschools available here are simply better than the competing public and private schools. Same professionalism. More caring and more emphasis on values we identify with. And then there is the whole bonus of giving a warm, positive basis to Jewish identity – for all types of families."[56]

"Jewish preschools helped us recognize that we wanted to have a Jewish family with a Jewish identity and be proud of it and to make our children understand why we don't have a Christmas tree."[57]

"Jewish preschool did as much for us as for our children. We made Jewish friends. It was a comfortable transition into the Jewish community."[58]

Most parents feel that Jewish preschool has added more Jewish content into their lives[59] and most continue their child's Jewish education in some form.[60] Furthermore, many parents report that they met many of their Jewish friends through Jewish preschool. These schools thus often serve as an introduction and gateway to the Jewish community.[61]

If you want your children to maintain their Jewish identity, then start at the beginning – choose a Jewish preschool that has quality Jewish content and role modeling.

CHAPTER 10

Consider a Day School Education

In Europe, Jews were victimized and often barred from mainstream education. When they immigrated to America, Jews found public schools of high quality that were open to all, and enthusiastically supported them.[62-63]

But in recent years, many – if not most – of America's public schools have changed dramatically, and for the worse. America's schools used to be the envy of the world. Now they rank among the *lowest* in the industrialized world.

The Paris-based Organization of Economic Cooperation and Development (OECD) does regular studies of education around the world. Results from the OECD's Program for International Student Assessment (PISA) of 2003 revealed that out of the 29 Western industrialized countries participating in the survey, the United States ranked[64] 23rd or 24th in math performance, problem-solving, and science, and 15th in reading. In almost all areas, the United States public school system ranked "significantly below average."

The deterioration of public schools is not limited to pure academics. When teachers were asked to rate the top disciplinary problems in public schools in 1940, and again in 1990, the difference in their responses was startling – even frightening:

Top Disciplinary Problems in Public Schools	
1940	**1990**
1 Talking out of turn	1 Drug abuse
2 Chewing gum	2 Alcohol abuse
3 Making noise	3 Pregnancy
4 Running in the hall	4 Suicide
5 Cutting in line	5 Rape
6 Dress code violations	6 Robbery
7 Littering	7 Assault

NOTE: In both instances, these were the top problems as rated by teachers. SOURCE: Alexander Volokh and Lisa Snell, Policy Study No. 234: School Violence Prevention, Strategies to Keep Schools Safe (Unabridged), (Reason Public Policy Institute (RPPI): 1998), introduction.

Students today confront an entirely different reality than students from one or two generations ago.. Many of America's public schools have serious problems with violence, drug use[65] and early sexual activity. Consider these recent statistics:

- 96 percent of high schools, 94 percent of middle schools, and 74 percent of primary schools reported violent incidents of crime by their students.[66] Over one third of middle and high school students don't feel safe at school.[67]
- Almost 50 percent of teenagers experiment with drugs before graduating from high school[68], with 20 percent experimenting by 7th grade. 25 percent of high school seniors and 14 percent of eighth graders used drugs in the last 30 days.[69]
- Approximately half of high school students reported having had sexual intercourse, including 65 percent of seniors.

68 percent don't consider themselves at risk of contracting Sexually Transmitted Diseases (STD's) and don't use contraception every time they have sex. [70]

- 36 percent of teens say they have engaged in sexual activity or felt pressure to do so when they didn't feel ready.[71]

Alternatives to Low Quality Public Schools

Many Jewish parents want to find a better environment for their children and avoid the problems of low quality public schools. What are their choices? Some move to areas with highly regarded public schools, while other parents choose a private school.[72]

Significantly, after examining the alternatives, more and more Jewish parents are choosing to enroll their children in Jewish day schools. In recent years, the growth of Jewish day school enrollment around the United States has been phenomenal. In 1998-99, fewer than 185,000 students were enrolled in Jewish elementary and secondary (high) schools in the United States. By the 2003–04 school year, there were 205,000 students,[73] an increase of 11 percent.

Considering that the overall Jewish population of the United States is both shrinking[74] and aging[75], why is Jewish Day School enrollment *growing*? The first explanation would seem to point to the Orthodox community with its high birth rates and near universal emphasis on day school education. Certainly, the number of students from Orthodox families in Jewish day schools has grown substantially.

However, Jewish Day School enrollment is increasing in <u>both</u> the Orthodox and non-Orthodox communities. Reflecting upon its 2005 census of Jewish education[76], the AviChai foundation reported that:

"Increasing numbers of day school parents are not Orthodox, and many adults in the parent bodies of [day] schools were not themselves educated in day schools."[77]

Similarly, at a symposium in May 2007 introducing a major new study, **The Impact of Day School: A Comparative Analysis of Jewish College Students,** Professor Len Saxe announced, "There has been substantial growth in both the Orthodox and non-Orthodox day school population."[78]

So why do Jewish parents – of all backgrounds—send their children to day schools? Four major factors motivate parents to choose Jewish day schools[79]:

- Excellent general (secular) education
- Positive values and peer group
- Being part of a community
- Jewish identity and continuity

While each family is different and there is a wide variety of day schools, most parents will choose day schools for a combination of these four factors. Let us consider them one by one.

Excellent General (Secular) Education

In many cases, the main reason why parents choose to send their children to a Jewish day school is the secular education that their children receive there.

Rebecca is an energetic and forthright freshman... She attended Orthodox day schools from first through twelfth grade...

When asked how well she felt her Jewish high school prepared her for college, she bursts out laughing and tells us "In high school I took 12 subjects—and had to do homework for all of them. Now in college, four classes are not such a big deal. Four classes and the work that goes with them are totally manageable."

It is very clear to Rebecca that she is doing well in her freshman year of college largely due to the intellectual discipline and academic skills she learned in her Jewish high school. In fact she feels that she has a distinct advantage over peers who did not attend a day school: "From high school I know how to participate in seminars and a lot of other first year students do not." [80]

Rebecca is not alone. Studies have consistently pointed to the high quality of the general studies programs of Jewish day schools. In city after city, and study after study, day school students have scored remarkably well in general studies.[81]

The most recent and comprehensive study on the subject, **The Impact of Day School: A Comparative Analysis of Jewish College Students**, was undertaken and published by the Cohen Center for Modern Jewish Studies of Brandeis University in May 2007, and validates that "day schools provide top-notch preparation for a broad range of colleges and universities, including those that are the most selective."[82]

Among the many findings of the report were that:

- Jewish high school alumni are accepted by "the full spectrum of institutions of higher education including the most highly selective."[83] Sixty-seven percent of day school graduates were accepted by their university of first choice, as high a figure as for comparable students who did not attend Jewish day schools.[84]
- Seventy-two percent are enrolled in colleges and universities in the top quartile of all ranked schools, according to U.S. News and World Report rankings. The Grade Point Average (GPA)'s of Jewish high school alumni are as high as those students from public or private schools, and the range of choice of majors is nearly identical.[85]
- Compared to all other groups, Jewish high school alumni[86] are "the most positive about the level of intellectual challenge and

engagement fostered by teachers in classes" and "demonstrate the highest academic self-confidence."[87]

Students who graduate from Jewish day schools go on to Ivy League schools at a rate higher than those from the competing private schools.[88]

A day school[89] in New York did a study of hundreds of its graduates from over 25 years of its graduating classes. The results were impressive in all realms.

For example:

- 98 percent graduated with at least a bachelor's degree.
- 31 percent went on to earn a Masters degree and a staggering 29 percent earned a Ph.D.
- 60 percent indicated they were on the Dean's List at their college or university. 39 percent indicated they graduated cum laude, magna cum laude or summa cum laude. 10 percent indicated they were elected to Phi Beta Kappa.

Jewish Day School graduates benefit in other, less tangible ways. Early exposure to a second language – Hebrew – opens students up to other foreign languages.[90] Also, Jewish Day Schools are typically smaller than other schools and thus the teachers and staff know the students and can give them more attention. Teachers are concerned about the children's development and encourage the children in all areas.

Positive Values and Peer Group

Academics are only one factor in quality education. As parents, we need to ask ourselves, "Which system will teach my child to be a *"mentsch?""* and "How will the school environment affect the way my child looks at sexuality, drugs, and other risky behaviors?"

A child is greatly affected by what he or she is taught in school and exposed to by their friends and role models. Few public or private schools even offer courses in values, and even fewer are successful at inculcating values. Professor Arthur Caplan, director of the Center for Bioethics at the University of Pennsylvania, explained that most efforts to teach character education in schools are woefully inadequate:

"Some people want ethics taught, but only if it is going to stay off of certain subjects like sex and drugs, which are probably—for most young people—the few areas where they can make moral choices", he said.

"And other people don't want it because they are afraid of being prudish or too conservative. And that's a mistake."[91]

It is not surprising that few schools have successful values programs. After all, which values are they teaching and who is supposed to be modeling these values?

A connection to one's religious heritage has an impact on people's behaviors and values. Teens who do not consider religious beliefs significant are almost three times more likely to drink, binge drink and smoke, and seven times likelier to use illicit drugs.[92]

Day schools graduates with more than five years of Jewish education are significantly less likely to binge drink than those who went to public schools.[93] Binge drinking and other forms of problematic use of alcohol lead to other risky behaviors and radically increase the likelihood of drunk driving, being in a car with a drunk driver, participating in unsafe sex and being exposed to unwanted sexual advances.[94]

Many parents value day school education because it fosters a strong sense of values in their children. By learning about Jewish values and being exposed to Jewish life, day school students have a greater chance of becoming ethical and moral individuals.

Typical values emphasized by day schools include respecting each and every individual, not gossiping, being involved in acts of kindness (*chesed*), feeling Jewish pride and joy, honesty and integrity, honoring parents and valuing family, giving charity (*tzedakah*), and more.

Similarly, many parents are attracted to day schools because of the positive peer groups that exist in the day school environment. Children are highly susceptible to peer pressure and need friends with good, healthy values if they are to successfully learn good values and behavior. Furthermore, a Jewish education strengthens the family by encouraging students to honor their parents and by offering access to traditions that help bond a family together.

Most Jewish parents want their children to learn these kinds of values, and a day school education provides consistency between the values of the home and school. Parents who enroll their children in a day school are gaining an active ally in their efforts to raise children of character and integrity.

Being Part of a Community

I know of a couple who first decided to send their eldest child to the local Jewish day school for a surprising reason: they didn't know anyone in town! They had just moved to the area and wanted to meet other Jewish people. They also realized that a few years of Jewish education could only help their son. They decided to try it and re-evaluate this decision periodically.

Within a short time they were very impressed by the quality of the school. They eventually enrolled all their children in day school and became enthusiastic supporters of day school education.

Day schools are central community institutions and open the doors of the wider Jewish community. Day schools also strive to develop a sense of inner community and can provide warmth, connections and support for families and children in times of need. It is not unusual for students and teachers to come to the aid of student-body families that may have a serious illness in the family or have suffered the loss of a loved one. Day schools also offer a wonderful support network of parents and create a sense of family and togetherness that can last for years after graduation.

One parent explained:

"Day school is much more than just classrooms and homework. The support we've found from school staff and the friends we've made among other parents, have made our day school the warmest Jewish community we've been a part of."[95]

Jewish Identity and Continuity

Many parents choose day schools simply because *day schools keep the children Jewish*. With rampant assimilation and Christian missionary groups spending millions of dollars annually targeting Jewish youth, a strong Jewish education becomes all the more imperative. [96]

A July 2004 study by the United Jewish Communities (UJC) found a strong positive correlation between years of Jewish education and Jewish identity and involvement as an adult. [97] Similarly, a May 2005 study by the United Jewish Communities concluded, "Today's children who are receiving Jewish education are likely to have stronger Jewish identities than the children who are not being exposed to Jewish education."[98]

The best – and some would argue, possibly the *only* – type of Jewish education that will keep Jewish identity strong throughout life is a Jewish day school. [99] Consider these findings from the National Jewish Population Survey (NJPS) of 2001. They focus on what is perhaps the main question Jewish parents have about their children's Jewish education: *Will my child stay Jewish?*

FORMAL JEWISH EDUCATION AND JEWISH IDENTITY INDICATORS

Jewish Connections as Adult → Previous Jewish Education ↓	Most/all closest friends Jewish	Ritual scale (out of five)[100]	Synagogue member	Being Jewish very important	Very attached to Israel
Day school: 7-12 years	74%	4.6	84%	86%	67%
Day school: 1-6 years	35	3.3	53	59	38
Supplementary schools: 7-12 years	32	3.1	56	51	36
Supplementary schools: 1-6 years	25	2.7	44	36	21
Sunday school: 7-12 years	20	2.6	36	35	12
Sunday school: 1-6 years	17	2.3	30	28	13
No Jewish education	7	1.8	12	16	12

NOTE: The list of education levels in the column on the left refers to how many years and what type of Jewish education individuals had when growing up. The list of Jewish indicators on the top of the chart refer to the results later on – how "Jewish-ly active" were these individuals when they matured into adults.

SOURCE: Steven M. Cohen and Laurence Kotler-Berkowitz, Jewish Communities Report Series on the National Jewish Population Survey 2000-01, *The Impact of Jewish Education on Adults' Jewish Identity*, July 2004, p. 10 (Table 1)

This table demonstrates that a day school education has a profound impact on Jewish identity later in life. Day school graduates are knowledgeable about and comfortable with Jewish identity and tradition. Because being Jewish has been a central part of their lives until graduation, it usually continues to be important to them after graduation as well.[101]

The impact of formal Jewish education is so strong that, historically, such education has been the central factor in Jewish continuity, as explains Professor Daniel Elazar:

"The history of the Jews has been a history of communities built around schools. They are the key institutions because they convey learning. Greek civilization survived for five hundred years after the Roman conquest of the Greek city-states because the Greeks, like the Jews, had developed academies and they could live around those academies. When those academies failed, Greek civilization disappeared. The Jewish people have never allowed its academies to fail."[102]

Impact on Community Involvement

A day school education has significant impact on later Jewish connections and involvement in the Jewish community. Of the graduates of one Jewish Day School studied by PEJE[103]:

- 96 percent were connected to the local JCC
- 90 percent contribute to Federation / Jewish charitable organizations
- 70 percent serve on boards and committees of Jewish organizations

Helping create this community involvement, and often resulting from it, is the fact that graduates from day schools are far more likely to make and keep Jewish friends as they go through life.[104]

Jewish Day School and Intermarriage

Intermarriage refers to couples where one spouse is Jewish and the other remains non-Jewish (marriages between a born Jew and a sincere convert to Judaism are not intermarriages). The 2001 NJPS report concluded that "Marriage to a non-Jew is rare among those who attended a Jewish day school... the more intensive the Jewish schooling, the lower the rate of intermarriage."[105] Furthermore, marrying someone Jewish dramatically increases the chances that Jewish identity will be preserved, and the close relationship between a strong Jewish education and in-marriage is a consistent theme in all major studies of the last decades. [106]

Two Generations

Parents who send their children to Jewish day schools correctly believe that they are keeping their children Jewish. In reality though, they are doing far more:

"Over 90% of parents who attended day schools through high school enrolled their own children in day schools."[107]

In other words, when parents choose an extensive day school education, they are virtually guaranteeing that in 20-30 years, their children will make the same decision.

Why Not Jewish Day School?

With all these reasons *for* a Jewish Day School education, it is not surprising that an increasing number of parents of all Jewish backgrounds are choosing to send their children to Day School. Yet, of course, many parents do not. Why is this?

The main concerns that parents have about day school seem to focus on five areas: (1) They want a high-level secular studies program; (2) They worry that day schools lack diversity; (3) They think day schools are just for Orthodox families; (4) They have practical concerns about location and cost; and (5) They are concerned that their children will know more about Judaism than they do.[108] Let's look at each of these in turn.

Question #1:

"I want my child to have an excellent general education and to be accepted into a top college. Isn't day school education a compromise in this area?"

Answer:

No. We dealt with this above. Most day schools offer general studies programs that are on a par with or better than most public and private schools.

Question #2:

"I want my children to be part of a diverse and multicultural world. Isn't day school education narrow-minded?"

Answer:

No. Like all of us, our children are heavily influenced by the values of Western society, including diversity and multiculturalism. Having a stronger Jewish identity actually *helps* people develop respect for others' identities and together work for the betterment of the world. Soviet Refusenik and former Israeli Cabinet Minister Natan Sharansky wrote:

"Only a person who is connected to his past, to his people, and to his roots can be free, and only a free person has the strength to act for the benefit of the rest of humanity."[109]

Aside from playing sports and being involved in other extra-curricular activities, Jewish Day School students study history, geography, and other secular subjects – in almost all cases by non-Jewish teachers—and are taught to respect other peoples and cultures. A recent example is the crisis in Sudan. Many day schools have had Darfur awareness & activism programs and many day school graduates have been at the forefront of the "Save Darfur" movement.

As mentioned above, day school graduates enter the best colleges and do extremely well there, "immersing themselves in all aspects of campus life and making friends through these activities."[110] The 2007 PEJE report found that day school graduates are:

- More likely than other students to be in involved in political or social action groups
- As likely to be involved in sports, performing arts and student Media
- Slightly less likely to be involved in fraternities and sororities
- Express a stronger sense of responsibility toward addressing the needs of society as a whole than other students[111]

Day school graduates attend the best graduate schools, and enter the professions of their choice, filling the ranks of doctors, lawyers, engineers, professors, and a host of other professions. While some parents fear that day schools may socially marginalize their children, the opposite is true. It is precisely because of their strong sense of unique personal identity that young Jews are sensitive to, and responsive to, the needs of those from diverse cultural backgrounds.

To summarize,

- Do day school graduates have a strong Jewish identity? Yes.
- Do day school graduates succeed professionally and socially? Yes.
- Do day school graduates have a respectful attitude toward a diverse world? Yes.

Question #3:
"Aren't day schools just for the Orthodox?"

Answer:
As noted at the beginning of the chapter, more and more non-Orthodox parents are choosing day schools. Yet, some parents still have the perception that day schools are for Orthodox families. As PEJE puts it:

> "That was true of the day school enterprise in the 1940s, 1950s, and 1960s. Since the 1970s and accelerating into the 1980s and 1990s, significant growth has taken place in non-Orthodox communities as well. In the past decade, **the greatest growth in day schools has been in non-Orthodox communities.** Increasingly, parents recognize that day schools provide an excellent education, and more and more communities and philanthropists recognize that day schools offer the greatest hope for Jewish continuity."[112]

One non-Orthodox Jewish parent said that she never even considered public school for her children:

> "Even though I'm not particularly religious, I'm Jewish. When they grow up, my children can practice however they choose, but they have to know where they came from to make an informed choice."[113]

To summarize, today, day schools are for all Jewish families. In fact, more and more non-Orthodox families are choosing day schools.

Question #4:

"What about cost and location?"

Answer:

Most Jewish families today live in or near major metropolitan areas and therefore have a day school – or several – within commuting distance.[114]

The financial burden of sending children to day school is indeed a serious concern. Because of their smaller student body, longer school days, lack of government funding, and high quality academics in both general and Jewish studies, day schools have significantly higher budgets than public schools.

The fact that some parents simply cannot afford day school tuition is a tragedy. Every Jewish child should receive a strong Jewish education, regardless of his or her parents' ability to pay. Considering the huge impact day school education has on the Jewish identity of its graduates, financial barriers are also self-defeating for the future of the Jewish community. The cash crisis of Jewish day schools is indeed one of the most worrisome and challenging issues in the Jewish world today. The Jewish community has not put enough focus on making Jewish day schools affordable for all Jewish families.

However, these dark clouds have some silver lining. First of all, many Jewish parents *can* afford day school tuition[115]: Day schools are no more expensive, and often less expensive, than comparable private schools. At the other end of the spectrum, low-income families usually benefit from substantial scholarships and tuition breaks.

What about those caught in the middle?

In the long term, businessman George Hanus has championed the "5 percent Solution" in which every Jewish person leaves 5 percent of their estate to an existing day school in their community. Within a generation, if widely adopted, this plan could have significant effects.

Already today, more and more federations and private philanthropists are supporting day schools. In April, 2007, New Jersey's largest Jewish federation, MetroWest, launched a $50 million communitywide campaign to support day schools. Local day schools will keep their own endowment funds while also benefiting from community and matching funds. Similar projects in other areas include a $45 million gift for excellence in Boston's day schools, a $50 million campaign to help reduce tuition in Chicago-area day schools, and $20 million for tuition assistance in Cleveland. Furthermore, an increasing number of schools are initiating tuition caps for middle-income families.[116] The Jewish community is moving in the right direction. Nevertheless, for many families, paying for day school indeed entails sacrifices and making difficult choices. But the benefits far outweigh the costs.

Question #5:
"Won't my child know more than I do? I don't know if I'm comfortable with that ..."

Answer:
Day schools are used to working with parents – from all backgrounds and levels of Jewish knowledge—to help make the transition positive, enriching, and comfortable for all involved. You are not alone in this: Many parents want their children to have the Jewish education that they never had. Parents report great satisfaction at their children being able to read Hebrew, etc. Some parents choose to use their children's education as a gateway to learning more about the holidays and other topics.

Final Thoughts

The investment in day school education is worth it. The quality of education that children are exposed to, the life-long friends they make, the values they learn, the pride in being Jewish they imbibe, and the work and study habits they acquire, are all central to who and what they will become. These factors form a person and contribute to their long term happiness and success far more than many other activities that parents invest in.

Ilene Sussman, Executive Director of the Day School Advocacy Forum (DAF) paraphrases the MasterCard commercial when saying: "You are providing a gift to your child, an investment in their future—it is priceless."[117] The single most significant investment a Jewish parent can make to ensure that their children remain Jewish is to send them to a Jewish day school. This book is full of many other important suggestions, and parents should not rely on any one factor alone. However, if I had to choose one, sending a child to day school would likely be the one I'd choose.

GETTING PRACTICAL

The more Jews know about Judaism, the more likely they are to remain Jewish. Therefore:

- Learn about and consider the advantages of a Jewish day school education

---

- Meet the principal of your local day school

- Speak to other parents who have chosen a day school education

---

- Show your children that you value Jewish knowledge

CHAPTER 11

Explore Youth Programs and Jewish Summer Camp

The advantages of day school education are overwhelming. They share the advantages of good private schools, offer a sense of community to students and families, and provide much higher rates of retaining Jewish identity.

However, in some situations, day schools are not feasible.

In some cases, parents may simply live in an area where there is no day school. Jewish boarding schools do exist and many schools have excellent boarding arrangements with local families; however this is not always feasible for all types of children.

Also, unfortunately, some parents do not qualify for scholarships and simply cannot afford to pay day school tuition. While there are usually tuition reduction plans and other solutions to this challenge, as mentioned in the previous chapter, in certain situations day school is not an option.

Finally, some parents don't realize the importance of a strong Jewish education until their children are already well-established in high school. For this reason, an increasing number of schools offer what are called *mechina* (prepatory) programs to aid transition from public or private schools, but these programs do not exist in all schools. When there is no *mechina* program available, transferring in later grades is often still possible and advisable, but not always.

In these rare situations where day school is not presently feasible, what can parents do to give their children a Jewish education?

Relying on Sunday school education or afternoon school ending around Bar/Bat Mitzvah is courting disaster. Most children whose Jewish education is limited to these options do not identify strongly as Jews when they mature, and many do not identify at all. A common theme in comments from adults who attended Sunday schools and limited afternoon schools as children is, "I attended for years and didn't learn anything." The number of hours is extremely limited, especially when assemblies, crafts, and breaks for holidays are figured in.[118] Research has confirmed this anecdotal evidence:

> Relative to those with no Jewish schooling, there are no consistent, positive impacts for in-marriage, ritual practices, and attitudes toward Israel associated with attendance at supplementary school for 6 years or less or at Sunday school for any number of years.[119]

If you are in this situation, what is your best non-day school option? You will need to focus on several crucial factors.

First of all, you must understand that Jewish education <u>cannot</u> end at Bat/Bat Mitzvah. Precisely then, the teenage years is when children begin to mature and think for themselves. This is when their views are formed. While your teen will continue to learn about other disciplines for another decade, if they stop their Jewish learning at age 12 or 13, Judaism will always seem childish to them – because the last time they learned about it, they were children. Part-time Jewish education that ends with the Bar or Bat Mitzvah has very little impact, as we saw in the table in the previous chapter. Parents must present continuing Jewish education as a given, like "regular" school. They need to know that being a knowledgeable Jew is as vital as any other part of their education. If your children balk at extra hours of classes, give incentives such as a mini-vacation with a Jewish angle (there are some great Jewish children's museums in New York, for example), or some other reward to keep them involved.

Secondly, the program you choose must have quality content and great teachers. Some programs are excellent, with a caring and inspirational staff and programs that keep children interested. Others are lacking. Do your homework. What do the students learn and how do they enjoy the program? Ask yourself – is this a place where my child can truly learn and grow?

Third, Jewish children and teenagers should have a peer group of other active Jewish children. After school, most children are not interested in other classes unless they have friends who are attending the same classes. In line with Supreme Court rulings, religious organizations in the United States are allowed to run religious, Hebrew, and other heritage-type programs after school hours on school premises. A number of excellent programs like this exist and the location and timing are ideal because students are already in the school with their friends.

Fourth, parents who do not send their children to day schools need to be even better role models than they otherwise would be. It is critical that you take personal responsibility that your family is growing Jewishly. You will need to model what is really important to you by taking your children out of school for Jewish holidays, getting more involved in the Jewish community, and learning more yourself.

Finally, I strongly suggest that you hire a private tutor for your child to supplement whatever Jewish and Hebrew classes they are attending. One-on-one learning is very effective in transmitting information and forming bonds. Tutors can often be role models to students. Twice-a-week learning sessions throughout teenage years can have a far-reaching impact, and are also usually quite affordable. Ask around for leads on where to find an appropriate tutor.

Youth Groups and Jewish Summer Camps

Youth groups also play a key role in the formation of Jewish identity. If students do not attend a Jewish day school, for example, they must be given environments in which they can form and maintain friendships with other Jewish children. One of the easiest ways to do this is through being active in a youth group. You can choose from a wide range of youth groups so you will need to do your homework to find which has the most inspirational staff and best peer group available. To gauge the quality of Jewish experience in any group, often the best method is to speak to parents who have children in those groups.

Overall, participation in Jewish youth groups and summer camps has positive effects. Consider the results[120] of a 2004 report:

INFORMAL JEWISH EDUCATION AND JEWISH IDENTITY INDICATORS

Jewish Connections as Adult → ↓ Previous Jewish Experiences	Married Another Jew	Most/All Closest Friends Jewish	Ritual Scale (out of five)	Synagogue Member	Being Jewish is Very Important	Very Attached to Israel
Attended Jewish Youth Group						
YES	75%	41%	3.3	58%	57%	37%
NO	49	16	2.3	28	27	17
Attended Jewish Camp						
YES	77	41	3.3	59	56	41
NO	46	14	2.3	25	25	14

> NOTE: The column on the left refers to which informal Jewish experience is being considered. The list of Jewish indicators on the top of the chart refers to the results later on – how "Jewish-ly active" were these individuals when they matured into adults.
> SOURCE: Steven M. Cohen and Laurence Kotler-Berkowitz, The Impact of Childhood Jewish Education on Adults' Jewish Identity: Schooling, Israel Travel, Camping and Youth Groups, (New York: United Jewish Communities, 2004), 11 (Table 2).

In summary, youth groups are important for all Jewish children, especially those who do not attend a day school.

Send Your Child to Jewish Summer Camp

Jewish summer camp can have a transformational effect on your child's Jewish identity. As seen in the table above, all indicators and studies show that Jewish camp alumni are far more active Jewishly than comparable Jews who did not attend Jewish summer camp. Jewish camp alumni are "*50 percent more likely* to join a synagogue, *90 percent more likely* to join a JCC and *twice as likely* to give $100 or more to their local Federation than Jewish adults who never went to Jewish camp." [121] Former campers are also more likely to marry other Jews and agree with the statement that "Being Jewish is very important to me." [122] According to the Jewish Camping Foundation[123], summers spent at a quality Jewish camp usually result in increased Jewish identity, affiliation, and practice. Finally, it is twice as likely for Jewish summer camp alumni to continue their Jewish education after Bar/Bat mitzvah than someone who didn't attend Jewish camp[124]. All good summer camps offer children wonderful life experiences. They spend time in the open, enjoy the water, explore nature and participate in activities such as sports, music, drama, dance and crafts. Campers gain independence (under a watchful eye, of course), build self-confidence, learn social skills, and form powerful friendships.

Jewish summer camps share these qualities and have one unique one as well: they provide a warm, inspirational and intensive Jewish experience. For many children, Jewish summer provides a unique, positive interaction with Judaism and Jewish people. For children who do not attend a Day School, Judaism often separates them from their peers and friends. At camp, Jewish activities help unite them with their friends. Over the summer, they live a fully Jewish life, where all their activities are done in a Jewish environment. There is no sense of disconnect between the Jewish part of their lives and the secular part of their lives.

Camps provide Jewish counselors and staff to act as role models. Shabbat is celebrated as virtually nowhere else in the world: in nature, around the lake, with everyone wearing a white shirt. Campers sing and dance together on Friday nights. They get inspired by stories about Israel, learn some Hebrew words, and feel free to "be Jewish" without feeling different or embarrassed. Jewish camps offer a comfortable environment where Jewish young people (no matter how 'religious' or not their families are during the rest of the year) can enjoy a warm, inviting Jewish community. At camp, being Jewish – and engaging in Jewish activities—is both fun and cool.

The American Camping Association reports that 63 percent of children who learn new activities at camp tend to continue engaging in these activities in some form after they return home.[125] While normally referring to issues of health, diet and exercise, the lesson for Jewish parents is clear: If you want your children to feel more positively about Friday night dinner, Jewish learning, or other Jewish activities that you are introducing into your home, Jewish camp is a wonderful ally. Once children and teenagers enjoy Jewish activities at camp, they are much more likely to want to continue them at home as well. Many parents are shocked to find that their children, who resisted Jewish stuff during the year, stand on the benches singing Hebrew songs at camp.

As a parent, you have a wide range of camping opportunities open before you, around the country and the world. In the US and Canada, there are over 100 not-for-profit Jewish camps and a similar number of privately-run Jewish camps.[126] These include specialty camps, travel camps, sports camps, and camps for children with special needs. Jewish camps accommodated 57,000 campers in 2000 and over 70,000 in 2008[127]. A typical Jewish summer camp costs between $500.00 and $1000.00 per week. Sessions run typically from one week up to eight week programs. In the last few years, there has been increased communal interest in and support of Jewish camping as a key player in Jewish identity. Many communities are partnering with parents to keep costs down and increase the number of campers.

Buyer beware: Not all Jewish summer camps are equal, though, in terms of their Jewish content. Some camps are populated by Jews but with very little Jewish content and a large number of non-Jewish staff. For a summer camp to have a significant Jewish impact, it must emphasize Jewish identity and knowledge. Quality camps provide excellent and safe overall activities, wonderful Shabbat atmospheres and programs, and an emphasis on Jewish values, songs, and celebration. Ideally, they should include some Jewish learning and offer positive Jewish role models.

College Years

Four years is a long time, especially for young people in their teens and early twenties. These are years when long term friendships are formed, attitudes shaped, and loyalties developed. Even students with a strong Jewish identity are in danger of losing their sense of commitment if they attend a college with no Jewish support system.

When the time comes for you and your child to choose a university, insist on one with a large and vibrant Jewish student community. Top tier universities exist with strong Jewish communities, so students can have their cake (top college) and eat it too (strong Jewish environment).

Do your best to encourage your children to participate in Jewish activities and programs on campus and to visit Israel with Birthright or other similar trip. Send the children Jewish care packages at holiday times. Sit down with them before they begin college and emphasize to them that as much as you want them to succeed academically, you also want them to "stay Jewish," developing Jewish friends and getting involved in Jewish activities.

Parental Attitude

As parents, our job doesn't end with the decision to give our children a strong Jewish education. A key factor in determining how successful our children's Jewish education will be is our attitude as parents. Most Jewish parents have a positive and healthy attitude toward their children's Jewish education, yet, sometimes we can make the mistake of sending contradictory signals.

We need to support and encourage our children's Jewish education at least as much as we support and encourage their general studies – if not more. If we are very clear about the importance of doing well in mathematics but never ask – and don't truly care – how our child's Jewish studies are progressing, our children will understand what is important and what isn't, and they will act accordingly. Similarly, we can't allow children to miss their Jewish classes for minor reasons when we would never do so with "real" school. If we send signals that Jewish classes are of lesser consequence, children will regard them as such.

Also, do not to undermine a child's Jewish education by comments such as, "Hebrew school teachers can't get real jobs." In one family I know, children learned about the gift and beauty of monotheism in the morning, where they were taught that most of the greatest minds in history were monotheists, and how Judaism brought belief in God – and the ethical morality that results from monotheism – to the world. When they returned home, they heard their parents say that people who believe in God were "weak," "weird" or "fanatical."

Similarly, the last thing we want to do is to convey to our children the wrong reason for Jewish education. When your child asks you why he or she needs to get a strong Jewish education, do not say, "To prepare your Bar/Bat mitzvah." When children hear this, it becomes difficult to then convince them to continue their Jewish education in their teen years because Jewish education has been defined for them as "Bar Mitzvah preparation."

So why *should* they receive a Jewish education?

As we discussed in the introduction, there are many reasons.

The world is beautiful in part because of its diversity. If small groups allow their unique cultures to fade away, everyone will end up the same – a loss for the entire planet. Furthermore, we Jews in particular are part of a unique and ongoing story. Our children need to be taught, first and foremost by us, that they have a special role to play in a very, very special story. More than anyone else, we as Jews need to understand the story and continue living it. We should tell our children that Jews need to know about being Jewish. Judaism teaches us about who we are and how to live a moral, spiritual and meaningful life. It connects us to our innermost selves, our history, our extended family, and to God.

Jewish classes should not be treated as an elective, where students can choose what appeals to them. Just as basic mathematics is not a choice, Jewish studies are not a choice. They are a blessing.

Final Thoughts

Jewish education is a process. Ideally, Jewish education starts young with a good Early Jewish Childhood Education program. It then continues into Jewish day school, and is supplemented by summer camps, youth groups, afternoon programs, trips to Israel and a positive Jewish experience in college. Each of these has a role to play, and each should be carefully considered. Your children's future Jewish identity largely depends on their Jewish knowledge.

GETTING PRACTICAL

Jewish Day school is, by far, the best choice for your child's Jewish education, but it is not always possible, and can benefit from supplements as well. Therefore:

- If day school is impossible, find quality supplementary programs AND hire private tutors

- Send your child to a quality Jewish summer camp

- Send your child to Israel for short visits or longer educational trips

- Insist on a college with an active Jewish student body and emphasize the Jewish connection during the college years

PART 4

Community

Children who grow up feeling connected to other Jews, both locally and globally, have a stronger chance of staying Jewish. Children who grow up feeling connected to their Jewish past have a stronger chance of staying connected to the Jewish future.

This last part of the book will help you create a sense of belonging to the Jewish People. You will also learn about the advantages of creating a family tree and the importance of involving grandparents in you children's Jewish development.

CHAPTER 13

Create a Sense of Belonging

A number of years ago, I was working as a tour guide for youth groups visiting Israel, and we were spending the morning in the Diaspora Museum of Tel Aviv University. Near the entrance was a small model made out of white plaster. Whenever I took groups there, I would cover the sign describing the model and ask my groups to guess what the scene is about. Jews from around the world, old and young, would identify the scene quickly.

See if you can too:

The scene is of a simple but elegant dining room table. The family is wearing attractive medieval garb, and the table is set with beautiful settings and wine glasses. The seats have extra pillows on them. At one end of the table is the father figure, with a scroll in his hand, listening intently. At the other end of the table is the mother figure, also with a scroll in her hand, also listening closely. On the third side of the table are two older children, perhaps 10 and 12 years old, sitting respectfully in their places. On the fourth side of the table, with everyone else watching, the youngest child is standing on a little stool and speaking.

As you've probably realized, the scene is Passover Seder night, and the child is asking the "Four Questions." In the many times that I've described the scene, many people guess the scene by the mention of the extra pillows, or the youngest child. Sometimes I need to add an extra detail or two in order to help people guess the scene.

The fact that Jews from diverse backgrounds all recognize this scene is quite impressive when you think about it: this small sculpture is based on a sketch from Medieval Spain, a place most of us have never been to. The people in the scene lived almost 1000 years ago and spoke a language few of us understand. They had no running water, no electricity, and no telephones, and the Americas still hadn't been discovered. It was a different world.

Yet, we recognize the scene because we have been one of its characters. We fit in the scene. We identify with it. Those people could have been our ancestors. I celebrate the Passover Seder, my ancestors did, and we're trying to make sure that our descendants will celebrate Passover as well.

Vertical Unity

When you think about it, what is it that truly connects us to our ancestors and descendants, after all? Is our connection just blood, just DNA, or is our link something deeper, more profound?

Blood lines do exist, but without even considering converts to Judaism (who are Jewish with no blood-link), how close is my genetic connection to my parents, after all? Let us take an example. Physically speaking, I am one half of my mother, one quarter of her mother, one eighth of her mother, one sixteenth of her mother, and one thirty-second of her mother. Go back just another generation (one sixty-fourth) or two (one out of one hundred and twenty-eight) and you'll get the idea. My connection to my great-great-grandmother is that I am physically composed of such a small part of her genes? Does this sound like a deep connection? If blood is our connection, then the connection is quite weak. Our connection to our ancestors is much more than ethnicity or blood.

Our real connections are Jewish ones.

We are all part of the same chain, the same story, the same tradition. If my ancestors were to hop in a time machine and visit me today, virtually every aspect of our modern world would seem very strange to them. They would be shocked by the telephone, computer, radio, car, MP3 player, modern clothing styles, and much else. They would likely feel very out of place.

However, some objects would make them feel more comfortable. The mezuzahs on the doorposts mirror the ones they had. The Hebrew volumes on the shelves include some of very same titles that they surely used (for example, the Torah and the prayerbook). The Shabbat candlesticks and Chanukah Menorah are similar to the ones they undoubtedly possessed. The Jewish aspects of my home connect me to my ancestors' homes – because they shared these aspects as well.

The little model from the Diaspora Museum in Tel Aviv shows the *vertical unity* of the Jewish people. We are in fact closely connected to all generations of Jews, past and future.

Horizontal Unity

A couple of years after college, I embarked on a road trip around North America. My parents helped me buy a used Ford Tempo, I filled the trunk up with books and tapes, and hit the road. It was a wonderful six-month long expedition, and I visited much of both Canada and the United States. I started in my hometown of Montreal, slowly worked my way down the East Coast to Florida, then to Louisiana and Texas. Eventually I made it to California, the Pacific Northwest and then the Rockies, Mount Rushmore and then home. All along the way I visited friends and family, stopped in on the tourist spots, and enjoyed the national parks.

In early April, I was in southwestern New Mexico, hiking in the beautiful hills that are marked by native American dwellings over a thousand years old. I had planned to be in Los Angeles with friends for the Passover Seders, but only had 48 hours to get there.

True, it was still possible to make it there on time, but that would mean skipping so many important things to see: the National Parks of southern Utah, Arizona, and, of course, Las Vegas.

I decided to change plans. I drove into the closest Jewish metropolis—Albuquerque, New Mexico, checked into a Youth Hostel, and sat down with the phone book (this was before the Internet). Before long, everything was arranged and it was one of the nicest Passover holidays I've ever had. Not only because of the songs, discussion, stories, singing, and great food. Even more impressive to me was the fact that they didn't know me a bit. I was Jewish and I was welcome. Instinctively, I knew that this was the case in whichever city I might find myself, anywhere around the world. I'd always heard about Jewish unity, but this was the first time that I felt it.

We all know how much Diaspora Jews care about Israel, feeling deeply connected to the safety and future of the Jewish community there. The feelings go in the other direction as well. For example, in 1976 a plane carrying almost 100 Jews was hijacked by Palestinian terrorists and diverted to Entebbe, Uganda. Israel sent in commandos to save them. Why? Because they were Jews. Also, when a few elderly Jews were discovered living in dire conditions and fearful of their future in Iraq following the Allied invasion in 2003, planes were sent to bring them home to Israel.

When Jews needed help in Argentina after the financial collapse there between 1999 and 2002, Jewish communities worldwide sent financial support amounting to almost $50 million dollars. When Jews in the former Soviet Union were being persecuted and barred from practicing their religion or leaving the country, Jews around the world organized and ultimately forced the USSR to "Let My People Go."

These are examples of the *horizontal unity* of the Jewish people. Because of the links we share with Jews around the world, we have automatic connections wherever we go. We may not always be aware of it, but in times of reflection (or crisis), we realize that we are deeply connected to Jews everywhere, no matter where they live or what language they speak.

"My People"

This sense of *horizontal* and *vertical* unity of the Jewish People can have an enormous effect on our children. When they feel they are part of a bigger family, and part of a story, they are very likely to want to stay part of that family and part of that story. They are very likely to want their spouse and children to feel connected to that same family and story as well.

So how do we as parents instill this sense of belonging in our children? How do we help our children realize that they are part of something greater than themselves? How do we ensure that they will feel connected – deeply connected – to the Jewish People?

Here are some practical tips:

Feel the Jewish Connection Yourself

If your Jewish identity is central to who you are, you will have a much easier time helping your children identify that way as well. Read, think, and reflect on why being Jewish is important to you. Demonstrate your connection to other Jews by being involved in your local community and being interested in what is happening to Jewish communities worldwide and in Israel. Make sure you have a circle of Jewish friends, and exhibit concern for the Jewish future.

Travel Jewishly

When you travel, travel Jewishly. Visit historic synagogues and Jewish tourist sites in Europe and around the world (you'd be surprised at how many there are). Bring Shabbat candles wherever you go. The unstated but powerful message is that being Jewish is not just something that you do at home or at synagogue. Rather, Jewishness is always with you. It is part of who you are wherever you are. Growing up with this attitude can have significant effects on how your children decide to live when they go away to college or move out on their own. If you are traveling without the children, make sure to take pictures and tell them about the synagogue you visited in Hong Kong or the Jewish communities you visited in South America – or Chicago.

In the same vein, I know people who order kosher food on all flights they take, even though they don't keep Kosher at home. Their reason is that they want as many kosher meals as possible to be ordered in order to help guarantee the availability of such meals for the rest of the Jewish people. By explaining this reasoning to their children, they send a more powerful message of Jewish unity to their children than a lifetime of High Holiday sermons!

Send Them on Jewish Trips

Teenage trips to Eastern Europe and Israel have had an enormous impact on participants. Start putting away money early for them, and present the trip as a unique opportunity, something that they should look forward to and work toward. Arrange for former participants to tell them how great the experience was. Going yourself shows them what solidarity means, and that we are all one people. If you can, offer to pay for a semester or Junior Year Abroad in Israel. Aside from what they learn in these trips, the subconscious effect is tremendous. What existed in Europe – and what happened there – is part of their past. What happens in Israel – is part of their present and future.

Make a Family Tree

Children like knowing where they come from. Explore your family's history and read up on Jewish genealogy. Let them know that they are part of something bigger than themselves, that they belong.

Many people feel that they can't find out much about their families. This is not usually the case. The Jewish Genealogy web site, JewishGen, writes:

> "With some research, it is possible to trace a Jewish family back many generations, even in Eastern Europe. Your genealogical search will be a very rewarding experience."

The next chapter gives more information on making a family tree.

Learn About Jewish History

Parents and children can all connect to their Jewish past. The Torah itself says, *"Remember the days of old: understand the years of ages past"* (DEUTERONOMY 32:7).

Why should we learn history? Many reasons exist. The most famous one is related to George Santayana's thoughtful comment: "Those who cannot remember the past are condemned to repeat it." There is, however, an additional, deeper reason to learn about one's past. Every individual at some point struggles with the basic question, "Who am I?" Understanding your past is crucial to understanding your present and future.

Consider this exercise:

> You have just embarked on a long journey. There are no exact directions: you were told that at each intersection you come to, a signpost tells travelers what lies ahead, what lies to the right, and so on. With the signposts indicating the way, you aren't too worried. With

time, the roads becomes less and less traveled and the space between intersections grows longer and longer. Eventually you come to a point that is completely deserted. It has been an exceptionally long time since the last road crossing. You are relieved to arrive at an intersection but distraught that the signpost with all the directions on it has fallen down on the ground.

How can you continue on the correct path?

With the sign down on the ground, how can you know where to go?

Take the signpost and stand it up straight. Then take the arrow that has the name of your point of departure and point it back to where you just arrived. The other arrows line up automatically and you'll know where to go!

People who know where they are coming from also know where they are going. But if we don't know where we are coming from, how can we possibly know where we are going?

In other words, history helps us understand who we are and where we are going. This is true at an individual level and a communal level as well. As Blind Czech historian Milan Hubl put it in Milan Kundera's **The Book of Laughter and Forgetting**:

"The first step in liquidating a people is to erase its memory. Destroy its books, its culture, its history. Then have somebody write new books, manufacture a new culture, invent a new history. Before long the nation will begin to forget what it is and what it was. The world around it will forget even faster."

Finally, there is something unique about learning Jewish history in particular. King Louis XIV of France, who lived in the seventeenth century, once asked Blaise Pascal, the great French Enlightenment philosopher, if there was any proof of the supernatural.

Pascal answered, "The Jews, your Majesty, the Jews."

Pascal understood that Jewish survival and impact on the world violated all the laws of history and represented something both unique and valuable. Learning about Jewish history opens the heart and mind to the wonder and miracle of Jewish survival and existence, and inspires a person to be part of this extraordinary people.

Bring knowledge of Jewish history into your family in an appealing way. Dates are boring. The best way to teach history is through stories, making children feel part of their people and their tradition.

Tell Family Stories

My father still remembers vividly where he found the Afikomen (the special piece of matzoh that is hidden) at the Passover Seder and was rewarded with the best present of his childhood: a new bike. The event occurred over 60 years ago.

Similarly, a generation later, I remember searching for the Afikomen for a long time, only to realize that my grandfather had hidden the matzah—in the matzoh box!

Did someone in your family tell you a story about your ancestors? Well, now it's your turn to tell that story to your children. These stories don't have to be about history-making or life-changing events. In certain ways, small everyday stories that highlight something about being Jewish are the best way to send a message about how Judaism has always been part-in-parcel of your family life.

Hold On to Traditions

Did your mother or grandmother cook a certain food for Friday night dinner or have a special Rosh Hashanah, Passover, or

Chanukah recipe? Let your children grow up seeing you embrace family traditions. They will get the message: that just like Mom & Dad are links in a chain, a delicious chain, one day their turn will come to keep these traditions alive. If your family doesn't have many traditions, you can always create a few of your own. See the section on holidays for more ideas.

Take a Chanukah Picture

Make it a tradition on Chanukah to take a family photo with your children and all your Menorahs in the picture. Take these photos out every year and have fun reminiscing and watching the family grow – all in the context of a joyous Jewish holiday.

Hopefully, they will come to think about who will be in their future pictures and will want their spouse and children to "fit in" as well.

Jewish Names

Jewish names can help connect a child to the Jewish people. The Talmud says that one of the reasons the Jewish people merited being redeemed from Egypt is that they kept their Jewish names. What is so great about keeping one's Jewish name?

In Jewish thought, a name helps define a person. By maintaining their Jewish names, they were indicating that they defined themselves as Jews.

Only a couple of generations ago, many Jewish immigrants to the United States couldn't wait to drop their Jewish identity and "be American." These could-almost-be-true anecdotes satirize what happened to the first generations that arrived in the New World:

A man changed his name from Cohen to Jones to Smith so that when he was asked what his name was before he changed it to Smith, he could say that his previous name was Jones.

Cohen and Rosenberg go into business together and decide to call themselves Jones and Jones. A customer calls and asks to speak to Mr. Jones. The secretary answers, "Which Jones do you want, Cohen or Rosenberg?"

Unlike these humorous examples, few Jews today are consciously trying to escape their identity. In our age, having a Jewish name can help a child identify with their heritage.

Close friends of ours recently had a baby girl. Not a particularly "religious" couple, they nevertheless chose a very Jewish name for their daughter—Michal. My wife and I were ecstatic for them, not just because of the new addition to their family, but also because their beautiful baby will have a constant reminder of who she is; her very name will automatically connect her to the Jewish people.

Some parents will feel comfortable giving the child a Jewish name as his or her only name. Others will want to choose a name that is Jewish, but one that isn't too conspicuous. Still others will give two names – a common American-type name and a Jewish name as well. If you choose this third option, try and use your child's Jewish name occasionally. Let the child be comfortable with their Jewish name and feel that it is part of their identity.

Learn Hebrew

As the Jewish national language, Hebrew connects us to Israel and makes Jewish tradition, prayer, and religious studies much more accessible and meaningful. It also links us to Jews around the world since they will also share the Hebrew connection.

A Jew who understands Hebrew feels much more at home and connected to synagogue, Israel, and Jews worldwide. Parents who don't read Hebrew can learn the letters within a few short hours. Bringing up children to know basic Hebrew gives them an immediate connection to Jews and Judaism wherever they happen to be.

Join the Jewish Community Center

Over 250 JCCs in the USA and Canada offer services in sports, fitness, culture, education, professional development, senior programs, and much more. Joining a JCC allows you to meet and interact with other Jews, find out more about programs that may interest you, and support local Jewish institutions.

Live in a Jewish Area

If you are moving or mobile, consider relocating to an area that has a significant number of other Jews. The advantages of living in a Jewish area include:

- A good number of the children' friends will be Jewish.
- There will be less pressure to celebrate Christmas. The children will feel normal celebrating Jewish holidays when other homes around them are celebrating them too.
- It will be easier for you to "make your family more Jewish" when many people around you are Jewish too.

Join a Synagogue

Synagogues are the Jewish community's centers for prayer and study. However, they also serve a social function in bringing the community together. The Hebrew word for synagogue, "Bait HaKnesset," means House of Assembly. By joining and getting involved in a synagogue, you can meet other Jews, find a positive Jewish peer group for your children, and become part of a community.

Foster a Connection to Israel

Jews always had a strong connection to Israel, even before the modern return to our ancient homeland. Throughout history, we constantly prayed for the welfare of Israel. Our holy texts discuss Israel in depth. Jews dreamed of the Holy Land and spoke of it often.

Today as well, one of the most meaningful Jewish connections many people have is their bond with Israel. Love and support for Israel keeps Jews together and often inspires Jewish involvement and dedication. For many, feeling connected to Israel is crucial to feeling strongly connected to being Jewish. How can we foster a close Israel-connection in our children?

Fortunately, creating a love for Israel is not difficult. Here are some suggestions:

- Let yourself love the country and the rest of the family will be affected as well.
- Have Israeli objects in your home. For example, a map of Israel, a charity box (pushka) for Israeli charities, photos and artwork of Israeli scenes, a "mizrach" pointing the way to Jerusalem, and so on.
- Learn about Israel and make it a regular topic of family discussions.
- Focus on the positives of Israel: the great miracle of our return, the ingathering of Jews from Europe, North Africa, and more recently Russia and Ethiopia. Read about the ancient stories that occurred there and the many struggles to return throughout the ages.

- When your children are old enough to understand, discuss the issues that Israel faces, explain why Israel is depicted so negatively around the world, write letters praising those who give fair coverage, and support pro-Israel advocacy groups.
- Send holiday baskets to Israeli soldiers and flowers and financial support to victims of terror.
- Direct your tzedakkah (charity) money toward Israeli hospitals and other charitable organizations. Get the children involved in raising money as well (for example with walkathons and other community activities).
- Learn Hebrew and have the children learn it as well.
- Buy Israeli products to support the economy.
- Have your family meet and interact with Israelis. Personal connections are very powerful.
- Attend Israel Day activities in your community.
- Eat Israeli food (pita, humous, shwarma, falafel, Israeli salad, bourekas, Moroccan pastries, and more) at home and at the local kosher Israeli restaurant.
- Keep an Israel photo album from your last visit.

Of course, the best way to build feelings toward Israel is to visit Israel. Traveling to Israel as a family can be a powerful Jewish experience that leaves a lasting impression on everyone in the family. Sending teenagers and young adults on Israel trips leaves participants inspired and knowledgeable about the unbelievable history of our people. They'll return full of Jewish pride and forever changed by the extraordinary bonding they've had with Jewish peers.

Visiting Israel has a significant impact on Jewish identity, in a variety of ways. People who visit Israel have much higher rates of staying active in the Jewish community. The following table outlines some of the effects of visits to Israel:

INFORMAL JEWISH EDUCATION
AND JEWISH IDENTITY INDICATORS

Jewish Connections as Adult → Have You Visited Israel? ↓	Married Another Jew	Most/ All Closest Friends Jewish	Ritual Scale (average out of five)	Synagogue Member	Being Jewish is Very Important	Very Attached to Israel
YES	80	45	3.5	60	67	53
NO	51	18	2.4	32	29	17

SOURCE: The Impact of Childhood Jewish Education on Adults' Jewish Identity: Schooling, Israel Travel, Camping and Youth Groups, Table 2, p. 10.

When people visit Israel for the first time, much of what they had previously learned takes on new importance. A spark is lit. The bus driver is Jewish as is the shopkeeper. Hebrew is a living language, not a dead one. The Western Wall is a real place. Jerusalem is a special, holy city. Israel trips are a vital part of Jewish identity.

Final Thoughts

One of the hallmarks of Jewish identity is concern for and connection to other Jewish people. The more your children feel connected to the Jewish People (in the past, present and future), the more likely they are to stay Jewishly-connected. Parents can and must foster these feelings of people-hood through activities, discussions, and visits to Israel and Jewish communities around the world.

GETTING PRACTICAL

Individuals who feel connected to the Jewish people are likely to stay connected to the Jewish people. Therefore:

• Get involved in the Jewish community

• Visit and foster a connection to Israel

• Travel Jewishly and send your children on Jewish trips

• Connect to Jewish historical figures

• Tell family stories and hold onto traditions

CHAPTER 14

Explore Jewish Genealogy

A person's past can make an indelible impact on their feelings of identity and belonging. Children who know about their family's Jewish history are more likely to care about continuing the Jewish link in the future.

Building a family tree is fascinating and fun. The process can help promote feelings of family togetherness, connection, and understanding through the generations. It also deepens children's appreciation of their identity as Jews by focusing on the many trials and difficulties our ancestors went through in order to remain Jewish.

Is the Information Accessible?

Genealogy is the study of family history. Many people think that there isn't much information available about Jewish family trees. Some Jewish genealogists point to several misconceptions that Jews in particular have that prevent them from doing research:

- People think that family names were changed at Ellis Island so that it is impossible to trace family history in Europe
- People think that no one (alive) in their family knows anything about family history.
- People think that their town and/or its records in Europe were

destroyed in the Holocaust and so there is no way of getting information.

In fact, these statements are often not true. Most names can be traced back, even when they were changed at Ellis Island (which, in fact, happened rarely). Furthermore, you can often find relatives – sometimes ones you didn't know – who can help you in the search. Finally, many towns survived and many records do exist even if the town was destroyed in the Holocaust.

The good news is that much research is already done. Jewish genealogy is very advanced and lots of information has been made available. As genealogist Dan Leeson wrote, for most of our history, "Jews have been genealogic aficionados, fascinated by the subject!"[128]

Jewish Genealogy and Children

Genealogy and children are a natural match, and the Jewish benefits of building a family tree have been too often ignored.

Two helpful verbs to know when you begin to learn about Jewish genealogy are "building" (as in a family tree) and "searching" (as in for relatives or information). Activities such as building and searching are ideal for young people and keep them interested and enthusiastic. For example, many children want to know how they are related to their cousins, or how many generations back a family knows its relatives.

By *building* a tree and *searching* for their roots, children are involved in a project that is fun and challenging, as well as educational. What will they learn? As you progress in your research, your children will learn about history, geography, sociology, government, immigration, military service, economics, and much more. Furthermore, you will be in contact with many branches and levels of government concerning census records, naturalization records, passenger lists, and military records as well as birth, death, and marriage registries. Trying to teach children about history and geography, for instance, in the classroom can be challenging because many children don't see how these subjects relate to them. What they see are boring dates concerning people they have never heard of in places they are not the least bit interested in. But when these issues revolve around their own family, suddenly the subjects come alive. If done with thought and understanding—and if your children are interested (not all are)—this family project can be a wonderful learning experience for them.

In a similar vein, genealogist Lauren Eisenberg had this to say about genealogy:

"Why do a family tree?"

... it is more than just a collection of names and dates. You can learn about yourself, your family, and society as a whole; it is a snapshot of history. It can serve as a tribute to the memory of those who have passed before us. In addition, we can get to "know" people whose life spans do not intersect ours.[129]

Jewish genealogy has many branches, each with its own methodology for getting information. For instance, current and recent family history will often depend on oral interviews. Older family information will be obtained through documents, often from foreign countries. Holocaust research necessitates much reading and research on the subject itself, as well as online research with Holocaust museums and Yad Vashem in Israel.

Jewishly speaking, the benefits of exploring genealogy exist at a variety of levels. Deepening connections to Jewish relatives both alive and gone, enhances children's connection to where they come from. Children who feel no connection to their Jewish family are more likely to "step away" from that heritage than children who feel a stronger connection. By researching the family, you will inevitably learn much about Jewish history, Jewish holidays, and anti-Semitism.

Parents should try to direct readings and research in a positive direction. For example, what was it like being Jewish then? What were they worried about coming to America? In Jewish terms, what do we have in common with previous generations? Why does Anti-Semitism exist? What can we do to keep our family's Jewish identity intact?

Where to Begin?

The first step a beginner can take is to read up on genealogy in general and Jewish genealogy in particular. Visit www.jewishgen.org for courses and book recommendations.

The Web

The Web has made Jewish genealogy much easier and has paved the way for beginners to understand how to begin searching for information. Some beginners' information is available in the Jewish Genealogy section of www.virtualjerusalem.com, but the most complete Web site is www.jewishgen.org. This site connects Jewish genealogists from around the world and has more information than most amateurs will ever need. The site includes a discussion group where you can ask specific questions that are not covered on their site, a database of over 200,000 towns and family names, and an every growing online *Family Tree of the Jewish People*, which already contains information on over one million Jews worldwide (relatives of yours may have already put up information on your family!).

Aside from gathering information for yourself, it may be particularly fun for children to submit information about your name and "hometown" to this site. They can feel that they are in fact building the Family Tree of the Jewish people.

"Start With What You Know"

One of the axioms of genealogy is to begin by recording all relevant information that you already know and start gathering facts about your parents and grandparents. As you move further and further back in history, you will have a certain path and natural procedure, rather than random bits of information picked up here and there.

Interviewing older family members is a great place to start. This can be done either in person, by phone, or in writing. Focus on finding out people's first and last names, where they were born, where they lived, and when they immigrated. Older relatives may have knowledge about dates and places, family events, customs, or stories that they never thought anyone would care about and so didn't bother telling. This is often the case. Record these interviews if possible.

Extend the circle by talking to friends of the family who might have information about your family, about European towns that you are interested in, or even about general socio-economic and religious factors that might interest you. "Word of mouth" is the single best way to find information directly relevant to you, is fun, and also helps strengthen Jewish family connections, which help deepen one's Jewish identity.

Yizkor (Memorial) Books

Yizkor books are devoted to the histories of specific Jewish communities, recording a town and its Holocaust victims. Most books describe the town's history, culture, institutions, and rabbis, and sometimes include a list of victims and survivors. Such books have been published for over 1,000 towns in Eastern Europe and are very helpful for discovering information about the towns. Many contain specific information on families from the town and may even include photos. While most are in Hebrew and/or Yiddish, some have English sections. The largest collection of these books is at Yad Vashem, Israel's Holocaust museum, but if you can't visit Israel, these books can form a part of your research. Once you find the name of the town in Europe that your family is from, you will be able to get in touch with others from the same town. Hopefully, they will have your town's Yizkor book. If not, perhaps you can start creating one together.

Visit Israel

A great way to connect your family tree project with your general efforts at strengthening your children' Jewish identity is a visit to Israel. Two main genealogical addresses in Israel are Yad Vashem, Israel's National Holocaust Museum in Jerusalem, and the Diaspora Museum, housed by Tel Aviv University.

Dedicated to preserving the memory of the Holocaust and its victims, Yad Vashem is considered by many to be Israel's most important museum, has a wealth of information, and its memorials are moving and thought-provoking. Genealogically speaking, its library contains over 100,000 volumes, including over 1,000 yizkor books. Its archives are unparalleled and well-organized (if you know the town name you are looking for).

Yad Vashem's moving "Hall of Names" memorial includes the "Pages of Testimony," an ever-growing collection of information about victims of the Nazis and their collaborators. Survivors and relatives of victims have filled out millions of pages, each including names of victims, parents, spouses, and children, as well as dates and places of birth and death, and contact information for the person submitting the information.

The Diaspora Museum in Tel Aviv was built on the grounds of Tel Aviv University with a goal of strengthening appreciation of Jewish life outside of Israel. Short movies, fascinating displays, and thought-provoking information make the visit a winner for anyone. In your quest for building your family tree, you and your children will enjoy using the museum's computers, with information on about a million Jewish names and families. Children will have a wonderful time looking up their ancestors and submitting their information for their descendants to look up some day. If you can't make the trip to Israel in the near future, you can access some of the information online

Perhaps the most memorable genealogical activity you can do in Israel is to meet your relatives. As your search progresses, you will discover more and more cousins, some distant and some surprisingly close, genealogically speaking. Most Jews today can track down relatives in Israel. Don't be afraid to call them and visit them. Israelis are a warm people and love meeting new relatives. These meetings are a wonderful way to help your children feel more connected to Israel, which is one of the great lynchpins of Jewish identity and to the Jewish people as a whole.

Final Thoughts

When asked about Jewish identity, most Jews will respond with something historical. They may mention the 2000 year old saga of our history, the Holocaust, or the desire to keep the Jewish people going. In many cases, however, they mention their own families' Jewish heritage. People like to know where they come from. True, some young Jews will not be interested in their family tree. For many young Jews, however, the research, the results, and the fascinating learning that results from Jewish genealogy will help develop their Jewish identities. They will feel a personal historical connection to their family's Jewish past and a heightened commitment to its future.

GETTING PRACTICAL

The more a person knows about their Jewish past, the more likely they are to care about their Jewish future. Therefore:

* Build a family tree

* Visit Europe, North Africa and Israel to "follow the trail"

* Learn about Jewish life in your ancestors' locations

CHAPTER 15

Get Grandparents Involved

In most families, grandparents can have a positive Jewish effect on grandchildren. Studies have shown that the more Jewishly-involved grandparents are in their own lives, the higher the percentage of their grandchildren who will attend a Jewish early childhood program, attend day school or camp, participate in youth groups, and visit Israel.[130]

Eminent sociologist Professor Steven M. Cohen of Hebrew University has conducted wide-ranging surveys of American Jewry, and asserted that

"many respondents... had very warm, positive memories of their grandparents, especially during holidays such as Passover... the influence of grandparents... (has) not been taken seriously enough by the Jewish community."

Furthermore, he continues,

"youngsters growing up are more susceptible to and open to messages from their grandparents than to messages from their parents... grandparents are among the major positive forces for Jewish identity."[131]

Clearly, grandparents are not a positive Jewish force in *all* families. In some situations, grandparents are not particularly interested in their Jewish identity. In others, grandparents can sometimes work against your efforts to strengthen your family's

Jewish identity. Every situation is different. Still, for most families today, grandparents represent a positive link to Jewish identity.

Use the Grandparents Advantage

Children love their grandparents dearly. After all, grandparents have many advantages. They get to give—and even spoil—without having to discipline. They can choose to be present at the good times and avoid the difficult times. These regular periods of "absence" from their grandchildren makes the latter's hearts "grow fonder," as the adage goes. Their time together is exciting for the children compared to ordinary time with parents. Also, many grandparents have more financial security than the parents and thus feel less pressure in their day-to-day lives. This often allows them more time, perspective, and patience with their grandchildren.

Not only do grandchildren easily love their grandparents, but they also can be deeply influenced by them. The constant giving on the part of grandparents can add tremendously to a child's feelings of self-esteem, self-confidence, and connection to the family.

Children love gifts, but in the long run, the greatest gift grandparents can give is themselves. Psychotherapist and author Miriam Adahan quotes one grandchild who reflected on her grandfather many years later:

"I never had the feeling he was giving up something he would rather have done in order to be with me. On the contrary, he gave me the feeling that being with me was the high point of his life."[132]

Adahan also asked her own daughter what she loved about her grandmother and was told that what stood out was "the little things, like her taking me out to eat—just the two of us. I'm special to her, special like no one else." Having one-on-one time with and giving unconditional love to grandchildren are key ingredients to a successful intergenerational relationship.

When possible, having grandchildren live in the same city as their grandparents is ideal. Being in close and regular contact with extended family gives a person a wonderful sense of warmth, support, and a sense of identity.

If grandparents live in a different city, well planned visits can still build a close relationship. When they are not together physically, grandparents can send small presents to show the grandchildren that they are never out of mind, make short phone calls to say "I love you," mail cards on occasions and birthdays, etc. All these strengthen this crucial feeling of inter-generational love. In many cases, the single most positive connection a child feels is to a grandparent.

How, you might ask, does all this translate to strengthening Jewish identity? Consider these three ways:

Role Models

The first way that a strong grand-parental relationship can help children's Jewish identity is similar to what we said concerning parents: "If they love you and respect you, they'll want to be like you." Therefore, if grandparents can build a strong loving relationship, *and if they themselves are role models of committed Jews,* there is a much higher chance that their grandchildren will be influenced in the same direction. In other words, the stronger the relationship, and the more the grandparents love being Jewish and are active in learning about Judaism and living it, the more their grandchildren will be pulled after them.

Thinking Long-Term

Secondly, if grandparents spend time with the grandchildren when they're young, building a close relationship, the children are more likely to feel connected to them—and want their company—later in life. Then, when the children have grown into teenagers and young adults, a beloved grandparent's advice and opinions on many issues – including Jewish ones—can have a real effect.

Will grandchildren listen when their grandparents encourage them to visit Israel? Will they move far away from family or want to stay close by?

By planting emotional seeds in the early years, there is a greater likelihood that the children will communicate with and be influenced by grandparents over the *long term*.

Adding Links to the Chain

The third way that a strong inter-generational relationship can influence the grandchildren Jewishly is more direct and immediate than the first two ways. This final method is *adding links to the chain*.

This idea is so central that it is worth some extra exploration.

What do sports teams (and their fan clubs), patriotism, class rings, alumni associations, and fraternities have in common? They all attempt to fill the basic human desire to be part of something.

We all want to fit in, to be part of a group. We do not like feeling disconnected or alone. Teenagers especially have a strong need to be part of the group and not to feel left out. However, this desire to be part of the group is also found among younger children in different ways: humans like feeling they are part of something.

Channeling this feeling was the goal of making a family tree and this is also where grandparents come in. Grandparents are the child's greatest and clearest indication of where they come from and who they are. Children love the link to the past that grandparents offer, for it connects them to something bigger than themselves.

They are no longer "just children" but links in a familial chain stretching back generations. Emphasizing the Jewish-ness of the grandparental-historical link reinforces to the children that the "Jewish stuff" is not just coming from their parents (who also tell them to eat their vegetables, go to sleep and stop watching so much television). Instead, Jewishness is central to their entire family, history, and identity. This message will make their entire Jewish education much easier, for they will see it all as part of who they are, not another subject in school or a household obligation.

In a similar way, grandparenting specialist Dr. Arthur Kornhaber emphasizes that one of the main grandparent roles is that of "living ancestor and family historian." Grandparents provide the link to "stories of relatives long dead, as well as passing on your family's ethnicity, ways, rites, rituals, and—hopefully—good cooking!" The effects of such a role are tremendous. Dr. Kornhaber explains:

When you provide your grandchildren with a sense of history and family roots by playing out the role of "living ancestor," and historian, when you pass on family ways, rites, and rituals, you teach your grandchildren to think in terms of "we" as well as "I." An individual child who thinks in terms of "we" feels that he is part of a historical continuum, and that makes the child feel secure and rooted not only to the past, but to the present and the future as well.[133]

Jewish parents and grandparents should pass on this idea of being part of a tradition. The story of our religion, history, and survival is crucial, but often personal connection to and responsibility for a family tradition is effective in stirring emotions of loyalty as well. The closer to home the better.

One grandchild reflected on his relationship to his grandfather, "Zadie":

By this time, I had come to know my Zadie, and I respected him, and liked him–and loved him. He was cheerful, always had a smile, a quip, a hearty greeting, a hug, a kiss–he was alive and vibrant and aware of the world around him. The truth is, for however shameful it may be, I loved him even more than my parents... My parents decided I'd be prepared for my Bar Mitzvah... Zadie showed up at my home, 7 a.m., mind you, with a pair of tefillin (prayer accessories) and announced that since I was now officially a man, in the Judaic sense, of course, I could start behaving like one. That is to say, before going off to school, I could put on my prayer shawl, tefillin, and pray.

This I needed like a hole in the head. But I so loved my Zadie–so deeply, and so without question or reserve–that despite the ignorant adolescent I was, somehow, albeit dimly, I perceived this man was not going to live forever; that perhaps his years were numbered; and I understood, however vaguely, I was my Zadie's last hope: dead though he would be, that I would carry on the Judaic tradition as it had come down to him from Abraham, Isaac, and Jacob, and maybe, maybe even pass it on to my children, and who knows, if I lived long enough, to theirs. So it was no contest. Without an argument or protest, or even a demurrer from me, we sat down at the dining room table, Zadie and me, and began to pray.[134]

At family gatherings and other times you can subtly make family history, and especially the family's Jewish history, a subject of conversation. Where did the candelabra come from? Which cousins have the other set? How many generations back does the antique dining room table go? Do you have a favorite piece? Tell them about it. Who was here for the last Pesach Seder? What do you remember about yours as a child? Does the family have any traditional recipes or customs? Did Grandpa hide the *Afikomen* for the children to find or did they steal it for him to find? Bring out the family albums and tell stories. Get grandparents involved to share their heritage.

Final Thoughts

The role of grandparents in forming a child's Jewish identity is often neglected. In many families, grandparents can be strong partners in your efforts to keep your family Jewish. They can and should be active participants in holidays, life cycle events and other Jewish activities. Grandchildren are usually beloved, which gives them great influence. Also, when grandparents are involved, children see that being Jewish is not only a priority for you as their parents, but an identity common to the entire family, passed on from generation to generation, and thus expected of them as well.

GETTING PRACTICAL

In most families, grandparents can have a positive Jewish effect on grandchildren. Therefore:

• Invite grandparents to participate in your children's Jewish development

• Have them talk about Jewish memories

• Share and cherish family traditions at holidays and other times

Conclusion

Two older Jewish men are sitting on a park bench. One notices that his friend is reading a radical right-wing, anti-Semitic paper.

He is shocked. "Why are you reading **that?!**"

His friend responds, "When I read Jewish newspapers, all I hear is the anti-Semitism, the terrorism, the assimilation. We are small and weak and getting smaller and weaker. It gets depressing and ruins my day.

On the other hand, when I read this stuff, all I hear is that the Jews are very powerful, growing stronger each day. It gives me a lift!"

With all the challenges facing the Jewish People today, both in terms of physical security and assimilation, reading a Jewish newspaper can indeed be alarming. In Western countries, the rates of assimilation are deeply troubling. Countless Jewish families are losing their heritage. The silver lining is that you are not passive observers in your family's Jewish future. With a little thought and focus, you can indeed keep your family Jewish. True, there are no guarantees in life. Some Jewish parents can do everything right and still watch their children walk away from their heritage. Fortunately, these cases are very rare.

Jewish parents who want their families to love being Jewish and stay Jewish can usually achieve positive results with a few easy and enjoyable steps suggested in this book. Raising children to love being Jewish does not require radical changes in who you are or what you do. All it takes is a desire to give your children the gift of a beautiful religious heritage and a commitment to add another link in the Jewish chain.

Endnotes

1   Based on a story told by Rabbi Jonathan Sacks.

2   Mark Twain, Concerning the Jews (Harpers, 1899) in The Complete Essays of Mark Twain (New York: Doubleday, 1963), 249.

3   *John Adams to F.A.Vanderkemp, 16 February, 1809* in C.F.Adams, ed., *The Works of John Adams* (Boston: Litte Brown, 1856), Vol.9, pp. 609-10.

4   Paul Johnson, *History of the Jews* (New York: Harper and Row, 1987), 585-87.

5   Heard from Rabbi Dr. Abraham Twerski, noted psychiatrist, author and founder of the Gateway Rehabilitation Center in Pittsburgh, Pa.

6   United Jewish Communities, The National Jewish Population Survey (NJPS) 2000-2001, (New York, UJC In Cooperation With The Mandell L. Berman Institute – North American Jewish Data Bank, 2003), p.7, Table 7.

7   Deuteronomy 16:14

8   Babylonian Talmud, Tractate Sukkah 51a

9   Maimonides Mishne Torah, Hilchot Daot, 2:7

10   In Deuteronomy 26:11. Note also: "….and you should be only joyous" (Deut 16:14); "The happiness that one feels on the holidays will enable him to increase his feelings of joy the entire year." (Masaas Moshe p.70)

11   Our happiness is deeply connected to our spiritual endeavors as well. As King David wrote: *Serve G-d with joy; come before Him with song* Psalms 100:2; "The Divine Presence comes to rest upon one only through his rejoicing in a mitzvah" Talmud Shabbat 30b; "Sadness is forbidden for it has many negative consequence"

(Sefer Chareidim) In addition to being happy, we are supposed to share our happiness. Talmudic Sage Rabbi Yishmael said that we should "greet every person with happiness" (3rd Chapter of Ethics of the Fathers)

12 Similarly, *"Only the lesson enjoyed can be learned well"* Babylonian Talmud, Tractate Avodah Zarah 19a

13 Likutei Aitzos, *Simcha*, #38. Similarly, contemporary author Rabbi Zelig Pliskin explained: "Whatever your attitude towards life and events, you automatically serve as a role model for others. By having attitudes conducive to happiness, you influence others to be happy." Zelig Pliskin, *Gateway to Happiness* (Jerusalem, Israel: Jewish Learning Exchange, 1983), 71.

14 As Rabbi Zelig Pliskin put it: *"Consistently make an effort to think thoughts conducive to happiness and you will be happy."* Pliskin, 49.

15 Tenuas Mussar 3: 202

16 Look at the section on Jewish Holidays for more information

17 www.littlefeat.net

18 'Children are acutely perceptive, and they quickly see through hypocrisy … [a child] won't take his parents seriously, because they aren't taking what they're doing seriously.' Yirmiyahu and Tehilla Abramov, *Our Family, Our Strength* (Jerusalem, Israel: Targum / Feldheim, 1997) 50-1.

19 Bruce A. Philipps, *Re-examining Intermarriage: Trends, Textures, Strategies* (New York: American Jewish Committee and the Wilstein Institute: 1997) , 13.

20 Dr. Mark Rosen, *Jewish Engagement from Birth: A Blueprint for Outreach to First-Time Parents* (Boston, Massachusetts: Maurice and Marilyn Cohen Center for Modern Jewish Studies of Brandeis University, 2006), 13.

21 For more on this subject, see my Why Marry Jewish? Surprising Reasons for Jews to Marry Jews (Targum, 2003) available at www. doronkornbluth.com

22 Dovid Orlofsky, "Bringing Up Baby: A Jewish Education Primer," in Doron Kornbluth, ed., Jewish Matters: A Pocketbook of Knowledge and Inspiration (Southfield, Michigan: Targum Press, 1999), 152.

23 Benjamin Blech, The Complete Idiot's Guide to Understanding Judaism (New York: Alpha Books, 1999), 125.

24 Maimonides, Mishneh Torah, Laws of Mezuzah: Chapter 6

25 see the Encyclopedia Judaica for beautiful examples

26 Deuteronomy 16:20

27 Cecil Roth, Studies in Books and Booklore; Essays in Jewish Bibliography and Allied Subjects (New York: Gregg International Publishers, 1972), 179.

28 Deuteronomy 16:14

29 Leviticus 23:40

30 Babylonian Talmud, Tractate Taanit 29a

31 National Jewish Population Survey (NJPS) 2000-2001, 7 (Table 7).

32 Based on an idea of Rabbi Dovid Orlofsky.

33 Tamar Milstein, "Parents Lay Out Lavish B'nai Mitzvah Fetes; Rabbis Cringe," Boston Jewish Advocate, November 13, 1998.

34 New York Magazine, Bash Mitzvahs, http://nymag.com/nymetro/urban/family/features/2343/

35 From http://djusa.com/barmitsvahs.html

36 Donin, 116.

37 Midrash Rabbah (Breishis 2:4)

38 Lawrence Kelemen, *Permission to Believe*, (Jerusalem, Israel: Targum Press, 1990), appendix. See also the 23 April 2000 edition of the Omaha World-Herald for more on this.

39 Genesis: Chapter 18

40 Full quote: "Rabbi Elazar would say, 'Hospitality is a greater thing than all the sacred offerings put together, for Scripture says, 'To do righteousness and justice is more acceptable to the Lord than offering.' ' " (Talmud: Sukkah 69)

41 Talmud, Mishna: Avot (Ethics of our Fathers), Chapter 1

42 Dr. Sylvia Barack Fishman, *Jewish and Something Else: A Study of Mixed-Married Families*, (New York: American Jewish Committee, 2001), 25.

43 "Rabbi Yehudah said in the name of Rav, 'One ought not to eat before feeding one's animal,' for Scripture says first, 'And I will provide grass in your field for your cattle' and then it says, 'and you shall eat be satisfied.'" (Talmud: Tractate Berachot 40, Deuteronomy 11:15)

44 Deuteronomy 6:4

45 Dr. Lisa Aiken, *The Hidden Beauty of the Shema*, (Judaica Press, 1997), 13.

46 Aiken, 17-19.

47 I am indebted to Rabbi Yehoshua Karsh for the inspiration for this chapter as well as many other valuable suggestions throughout the book.

48 Elizabeth Barrett Browning, **Aurora Leigh**, Seventh Book.

49 I am indebted to Ilene Vogelstein, *Director of the Jewish Early Childhood Education Partnership* and the Coordinator of the Early Childhood Department at CAJE, for her invaluable help in formulating many of the ideas in this section.

50   There are currently approximately 125,000 children in the U.S. enrolled in early childhood Jewish educational programs (0-5 years of age), constituting between 20-25 percent of the Jewish children in the US. Eli Schaap, *Early Childhood Jewish Education and Profiles of its Educators: The Number of Students and Teachers Within Jewish Education in the United States,* http://www.caje.org/earlychildhood/ec-survey04.pdf)

51   Rosen, 51. Based on the landmark From Neurons to Neighborhoods: The Science of Early Childhood Development. For more information on the subject, visit www.caje.org

52   Talmud Avot de Rabbi Natan 24.

53   "While positively disposed to a school's Jewish content, most families were not primarily concerned with providing a Jewish education for their children." Pearl Beck, *Jewish Preschools as Gateways to Jewish Life: A Survey of Jewish Preschool Parents in Three Cities,* (Baltimore, Maryland: Ukeles Associates, November 2002), introduction.

54   "87 percent of the parents reported being "very satisfied," the highest rating, with the school as a whole, while 91 percent reported being "very satisfied" with the Jewish programming." Beck, 9.

55   As one preschool mother said: "There is just a connection – you can't explain it – that you have when you are around another group of Jewish women, even if in the playgroup you never say anything about Judaism or whatever. There was just still some connection that we all had." Rosen, 32.

56   Private interview.

57   Beck, 22.

58   Private interview.

59   Beck, 20.

60 "Upon graduating from the Jewish preschools, the overwhelming majority (76 percent) of the interviewed families continued their children's Jewish education." Beck, 12.

61 Beck, 24

62 My thanks to Ilene Sussman, Executive Director of the Day School Advocacy Forum (DAF) for her critique and excellent suggestions in this chapter. Rabbi Michael Cytrin also offered excellent ideas and made several important corrections.

63 "Jews perceived them as an entree to America itself and supported them as a patriotic duty. Thus, while the Catholic church looked down on the public school as a symbol of much of what was wrong with America, and therefore set up its own system of parochial school education, Jews wholeheartedly supported and even idealized public education as a symbol of America's promise." Professor Jonathan Sarna in Fishman p.37

64 Organization of Economic Cooperation and Development, Program for International Student Assessment (PISA) of 2003, http://www.nces.ed.gov/surveys/PISA/datafiles.asp, Tables 1 and 4

65 The National Center on Addiction and Substance Abuse at Columbia University, www.casacolumbia.org.

66 http://nces.ed.gov/pubs2007/2007302rev.pdf, Table 1. Statistics from 2003. Violent incidents include rape, sexual battery other than rape, physical attack or fight with or without a weapon, threat of physical attack with or without a weapon, and robbery with or without a weapon. This does not include theft, possession of a firearm or explosive device, possession of a knife or sharp object, distribution of illegal drugs, possession or use of alcohol or illegal drugs, and vandalism. Similarly, in 2003, 41 percent of high schools report "unwanted gang activities. U.S. Department of Education School Survey on Crime and Safety: 2003–04, *Crime, Violence, Discipline, and Safety in U.S. Public Schools*, Table 5, http://nces.ed.gov/pubs2007/2007302rev.pdf. Furthermore, in 2003, over 78 percent of campus-based police officers reported

having taken a weapon away from a student on campus. National Association of School Resource Officers, *July 2004 Conference Questionnaire Results*, http://www.schoolsafety.us.

67   National School Safety Center, Review of School Safety Research, **http://www.schoolsafety.us/pubfiles/school_crime_ and_violence_statistics.pdf**, 9. Approximately 43 percent of high school boys think that it's permissible to hit or threaten a person who makes them angry. Nineteen percent of girls agreed.

68   National Institute on Drug Abuse National Institutes of Health, Marijuana: Facts Parents Need To Know, Revised, http://www. mccordcenter.com/facts/marijuna%20-%20facts%20parents%20 need%20to%20know.pdf

69   National Institute on Drug Abuse. Studies show that the younger a child is who uses marijuana, the more likely he or she will become a drug user as an adult. Kaiser Family Foundation, http:// www.kff.org.

70   http://www.teenpregnancy.org/resources/reading/fact_sheets/ default.asp; www.kff.org

71   www.kff.org. Over 40 percent of teens say they feel personally pressured about sex and intimate relationships.

72   Although many of these schools are affiliated with a denomination of Christianity, adding a host of problems for Jewish families.

73   AviChai, *A Census of Jewish Day Schools in the United States (2003-04)*, www.avichai.org.

74   The National Jewish Population Survey from 2001 (Table 1) revealed a Total Jewish Population of 5.2 million, compared to 5.5 million in 1991. This constitutes a 5.5 percent decrease, despite considerable immigration.

75   That is to say, there are fewer children in the overall Jewish population: "The American Jewish population is older than the Jewish population ten years ago....The Jewish population will

probably continue to age in the years to come..." NJPS 2000-2001, 2-3.

76 Avichai, The Current Moment in Jewish Education, www.avichai.org.

77 Ibid, 18. Interestingly, the report found that "frequently, their public and supplementary Hebrew school experiences are in fact the motivating factor in choosing a day school. One couple explained that their strong bias in favor of day schools was a result of the fact that both of them had gone to public schools and had "unhappy" Hebrew school experiences. "My observation was that [afternoon school] hadn't gotten better; it had gotten worse since I was a kid."

78 Partners for Excellence in Jewish Education (PEJE), *The Impact of Day School: A Comparative Analysis of Jewish College Students*, www.peje.org (Video of Symposium).

79 Some of the ideas here were inspired by Matatia Chetrit's article called A Better Chance in Life: The Ten Advantages of a Jewish Education. The article is available at http://www.torahchildren.org.

80 Fern Chertok, et al, *The Impact of Day School: A Comparative Analysis of Jewish College Students*, (Boston, Massachusetts: Maurice and Marilyn Cohen Center for Modern Jewish Studies of Brandeis University, May 2007), 11-17.

81 An organization called Partners for Excellence in Jewish Education is an excellent repository for information on the day school movement. Visit www.peje.org for up-to-date material, and ask your local day school for information on its general studies program.

82 *The Impact of Day School*, 2.

83 Ibid.

84 *The Impact of Day School*, 15.

85 *The Impact of Day School*, 19.

86 Including those from non-Orthodox backgrounds.

87 *The Impact of Day School*, 2.

88 www.peje.org

89 www.peje.org

90 "Recent Studies demonstrate that bilingualism enhances academic achievement and overall language proficiency, and positively correlates with the ability to formulate scientific hypotheses, cognitive flexibility, deductive reasoning skills in math, meta-linguistic abilities, and better scores on reading. Maria Estela Brisk, *Bilingual Education: From Compensatory to Quality Schooling*, (Mahwah: Lawrence Erlbaum Associates, 2006), 82 in Scott Shay, *Getting Our Groove Back – How to Energize American Jewry* (New York: Devorah, 2007), 85 (footnote #6).

91 "Teens and Religion", Washington Post, June 1, 2004, A12.

92 National Center on Addiction and Substance Abuse (CASA), *"So Help Me God: Substance Abuse, Religion and Spirituality,"* November 2001.

93 "Wechsler, Dowdall, Davenport, and Rimm (1995) define binge drinking as having five drinks for men and four drinks for women, and the rates of students engaging in this excessive use of alcohol (over half of men and about one-third of women) have remained steady over the last decade (Wechsler and Isaac, 1992; Wechsler, Lee, Kuo, and Lee, 2000) in *The Impact of Day School*, 29.

94 *The Impact of Day School*, 29. Based on studies by Wechsler and Isaac (1992), Meilman (1993), and Wechsler, Moeykens, Davenport, Castillo, and Hansen (1995)

95 www.peje.org

96 From www.jewsforjudaism.org. For instance, each year, over 600 different missionary groups spend over $200 million worldwide

toward converting Jews. It is estimated that more than 500,000 Jews have succumbed to their efforts.

97 Steven Cohen and Laurence Kotler-Berkowitz, *The Impact of Childhood Jewish Education on Adults' Jewish Identity*, (New York: United Jewish Communities, 2004), 10. Many studies confirm this strong correlation. For instance, a 1993 study by the AviChai Foundation found a positive relationship between the number of years of Jewish schooling and several Jewish outcome variables. Also, *Jewish Involvement of the Baby Boom Generation*, Mordechai Rimor and Elihu Katz (Louis Guttman Israel Institute). Consistent results with a 1994 study by the Mandel Institute for the Advanced Study and Development of Jewish Education was based on the famous 1990 NJPS data. It found that "the longer and more intensive the Jewish training, the more likely people are to be committed to and practice Judaism." See also *The Power of Jewish Education*, Seymour Martin Lipset,57.

9 Laurence Kotler-Berkowitz, *The Jewish Education of Jewish Children: Formal Schooling, Early Childhood Programs and Informal Experiences.* (New York: United Jewish Communities, 2005).

99 Compared to many other factors, "in general, attendance at a day school seven years or more exerts the most powerful positive impact on Jewish identity." Steven M. Cohen and Laurence Kotler-Berkowitz, 10. Many other studies have verified these results. For instance: "The Jewishness Quotient of Jewish Day School Graduates: Studying the Effect of Jewish Education on Adult Jewish Behavior," Azrieli Graduate Institute, 1994 found that "extensive" Jewish day school education is the single most important factor in the formation of strong Jewish identities."

100 How many Jewish traditions do they keep, in comparison? Do they attend a Passover Seder? Commemorate Yom Kippur? Celebrate Chanukah?

101 *The Impact of Jewish Day School*, 2.

102 Daniel Elazar, *People and Polity : The Organizational Dynamics of*

World Jewry, (Detroit: Wayne State University Press, 1989), 31.

103 www.peje.org

104 Ibid.

105 National Jewish Population Survey, 2000-2001, 18.

106 See also: "The Jewish-ness Quotient of Jewish Day School Graduates: Studying the Effect of Jewish Education on Adult Jewish Behavior," (New York: Azrieli Graduate Institute, 1994). For a local study, see the Jewish Education Council of Montreal's 1998 study entitled "The Jewish High School Experience: Its Implications for the Evolution of Jewish Identity in Young Adults" which compared Jewish graduates of day schools with Jewish graduates of non-Jewish high schools, and found: *"Graduates of Jewish high schools are significantly less likely to intermarry than Jewish graduates of other high schools."*

107 Jack Wertheimer, *Linking the Silos: How to Accelerate the Momentum in Jewish Education Today (The Current Moment in Jewish Education)*, (New York: AviChai, 2005), 9.

108 Also, some parents strongly believe in the principle of supporting public schools. Note, however, that our taxes support the public school system whether a child attends or not (and not attending may even improve the student-teacher ratio!)

109 www.peje.org

110 *The Impact of Day School*, 30. On page 28 the report adds that: *"the college social networks of Jewish high school alumni are overwhelmingly comprised of new friendships"*

111 Ibid., 39. See also Tables 12 and 13

112 www.peje.org.

113 Kelly Korbin, "Day School: Pros and Cons," *Jewish Independent of Greater Vancouver*, Aug. 25, 2006.

114 Boarding is also an option for some families.

115 Note that Jews have the highest annual income of any religious or ethnic group that is surveyed. Jews also have fewer children than other groups, resulting in even more disposable income. For info on the number of children born, see Table 4 and Table 5 of the NJPS 2000-2001 report, p.4 The median household income of the Jewish population is about $54,000, which is higher than the approximately $42,000 median for all U.S. households reported by the Census Bureau. (NJPS 2000-2001, 6). The same is true in Canada.

116 Jewish Telegraph Agency, www.jta.org, May 2, 2007.

117 In a private correspondence

118 Donin, 61.

119 Cohen, 14.

120 Note: The column on the left refers to which informal Jewish experience is being considered. The list of Jewish indicators on the top of the chart refers to the results later on – how 'Jewish-ly active' were these individuals when they matured into adults. THIS IS A REPEAT OF THE NOTE IN ABOVE TABLE

121 www.jewishcamping.org, based on studies from Atlanta, Denver, Delaware and national studies including but not limited to Amy Sales and Professor Leonard Saxe *How Goodly Are Thy Tents: Summer Camps as Jewish Socializing Experiences*, (Boston: Brandeis University Press, 2003).

122 Ibid. Sociologist Steven M. Cohen found that 66 percent of people who attended Jewish camps considered their Jewish identity "very important," as opposed to 29 percent of Jewish adults who did not.

123 www.jewishcamping.org, based on Sales and Saxe.

124 From Gary Rosenblatt, The Jewish Week, June 23, 2006

125 www.acacamps.org

126 Out of over 10,000 camps in the USA

127 Out of approximately 10 million campers in the USA

128 From jewishgen.org

129 www.jewishgen.org

130 *Linking the Silos*, 11.

131 Steven M. Cohen, General Assembly, November, 2003. See also similar conclusions in Steven Cohen and Arnold Eisen, *The Jew Within: Self, Family, and Community in America* (Indianapolis, Indiana: Indiana University Press, 2000).

132 Miriam Adahan,_*The Miriam Adahan Handbook: Living With Children* (Jerusalem, Israel: Targum, 1998), 18.

133 www.grandparenting.org

134 Ibid.

MORE FROM K'HAL PUBLISHING

Rosh Hashanah Yom Kippur Survival Kit

If you, or someone you know, spends the High Holy Day Services looking for the nearest exit—this is the book you have been looking for. This award-winning classic is a fun, friendly, spiritual, and insightful guide to all the central themes, concepts, and prayers of the holidays.

Beyond Survival: A Journey to the Heart of Rosh Hashanah, Its Prayers, and Life

Whether this is your third Rosh Hashanah or your thirtieth, Beyond Survival will take you on a journey to new vistas of insight and inspiration. This book does more than just explain concepts, it guides you along a path of personal discovery and spiritual growth.

Remember My Soul: What To Do In Memory of a Loved One

Lori Palatnik has written a thoughtful, sensitive, enlightening, and comforting guide for people who have lost a loved one. This book has helped thousands discover how the rich wisdom of Jewish tradition can help one not only cope, but also discover hidden layers of meaning—even in life's most difficult hour.

Inspiring Days

A collection of writings from a wide range of gifted educators, spiritual mentors, and writers. Reveals the great depth within Rosh Hashanah, Yom Kippur, Sukkot, and more.

Inspiring Lights

Another collection of remarkable essays that make the spiritual and intellectual lights of Chanukah shine brighter than ever.

Online store: www.afikimfoundation.org • 212-791-7450

About the Author

Doron Kornbluth is a bestselling author, widely sought after speaker and highly regarded Jewish Family Coach. Over the last decade he has taught, inspired, motivated and guided thousands of people in Israel, Europe, Canada and the US on a wide variety of issues related to Jewish identity and the Jewish family. His uniquely inspirational and humorous *Why Be Jewish* and *Jewish Pride* seminars are smash hits with college students, young couples and parents of all ages. His free e-newsletter is enjoyed by thousands of Jewish parents and grandparents.

Raising Kids to Love Being Jewish is the outgrowth of over fifteen years of teaching and counseling and years of intensive research. For years, parents who have attended his Raising Kids to Love Being Jewish seminar have been asking for a book—and now it's here.

Doron lives in Jerusalem and together with his wife Sarah, is actively involved in raising his own Jewish family. You can find him at www.doronkornbluth.com.